For all the Latina engineering and computing students out there, those who've crossed my path and those who haven't, this one's for you.

Contents

Foreword

The increased participation and success of Latinas in computing has been a lifelong passion of mine, and it was the motivation for founding the Computing Alliance of Hispanic-Serving Institutions (CAHSI). Involving people with different perspectives, experiences, and disciplinary knowledge in solving problems is critical for our nation's ability to innovate and compete in a global economy. Unfortunately, the trends in the numbers of graduates with baccalaureate and advanced degrees who enter the computing and engineering workforce are insufficient to meet current and future national needs. Indeed, computing is the least diverse field of all STEM (science, technology, engineering, and mathematics) disciplines, and it's imperative that we work as a collective to increase the number of Latinx, particularly Latinas, in computing. This is the role of CAHSI.

The dearth of literature on Hispanic student success in computing, especially Latinas, hinders higher education's ability to strategically plan and make informed decisions that can accelerate systemic change. Dr. Rodriguez's book provides the needed compendium of research on Latinas and methodically outlines how such research translates into practice.

A point raised in the book is on how identity drives Latinas' work, interactions, and motivation and, on the contrary, how it can suppress Latinas' ability to genuinely express themselves. Dr. Rodriguez emphasizes the importance of taking asset-based and disciplinary approaches to build Latinas' sense of belonging and identity in computing and engineering by capitalizing on their values and experiences. Another key point revolves around the unique context associated with each institution of higher education, including intersectionality perspectives, which administrators and practitioners must consider as they seek improvements to organizational structures and behaviors.

Dr. Rodriguez makes a case that *what needs to be done*, and *how it is done*, must be considered from the viewpoints of the individual, community, family, peers, staff, faculty, and administrators. Her book enhances the reader's understanding of why so few Latinas are in the computing and engineering fields and guides the reader toward organizational change and shifts in faculty mindsets. She skillfully captures the why, what, and how through storytelling, research, practice, advice, and action planning. *Supporting Latina Students in Engineering and Computing* is a must read for changemakers dedicated to accelerating representation of Latinas in these fields.

Dr. Ann Quiroz Gates
Senior Advisor to the Provost on Strategic STEM Initiatives and Executive Director of the Computing Alliance of Hispanic-Serving Institutions (CAHSI)
The University of Texas at El Paso

Preface

Why am I compelled to write? Because the writing saves me from this complacency I fear. Because I have no choice.

–Gloria Anzaldúa[1]

The prospect of writing a book was not originally part of my intended academic trajectory. The daunting endeavor of writing a book entails an immense investment of intellectual energy and emotional dedication. However, the juncture at which I now find myself compels me to write and share what I have learned. Gloria Anzaldúa's words resonate with me deeply. As a tenured professor in engineering education at Virginia Tech, entrusted with the rights, privileges, and responsibilities associated with this position, I sensed a calling to document the insights gleaned from over a decade of researching engineering and computing identity among Latina students and make them available to equity-minded practitioners who want to support these students.

PURPOSE OF THE BOOK

The purpose of this book is to use a research-to-practice approach to take what we know about the elements of engineering and computing identity for Latina students and translate this knowledge into a holistic approach that enhances identity and supports equitable outcomes. This book is unapologetically written for equity-minded practitioners. It cannot be all things to all people. With that in mind, I am writing this book for those of you who are committed to the uplift and success of Latina students and who, through your work, seek to see that all Latina students have the opportunity to see themselves as engineers and computer scientists. The equity-minded practitioner audience may include individuals responsible for the teaching, advising, and support of Latina students as they matriculate to and through higher education within engineering and computing. Equity-minded practitioners will want to read this book because it is research informed and accessible and can help you put learning into immediate action in classrooms and on campuses. It provides concrete strategies for enhancing engineering and computing identity for Latina students in higher education. While efforts to address issues of diversity, equity, and inclusion (DEI) in STEM more broadly have been customary over the years, there are increasing calls for discipline-specific approaches, as echoed in the American Association for the Advancement of Science (AAAS) report *Levers for Change*, which examines the potential for change in areas such as engineering and computing.[2] Thus, this book seeks to provide nuanced strategies to disrupt disciplinary processes and cultures within engineering and computing.

The chapters are meant to speak directly to equity-minded practitioners, including a discussion of how we might use Chicana feminist approaches to rethink engineering and computing identity and to speak more directly to the experiences, values, and desires of Latina students. Chicana feminism was not a happenstance choice; my choice is unapologetically concerned with ensuring that our approaches to engineering and computing identity are asset based, sociohistorically centered, and rooted in the belief that identities are interwoven, fluid, and dynamic. This choice for a Chicana feminist approach is also firmly tied to the need for our fields to resist against the blatant and more subtle forms of white supremacy and oppression that threaten to derail our efforts. The chapters provide suggestions for how to create the needed supports and relationships for a Chicana feminist–informed engineering and computing identity. The book also provides guidance on how we as educators can engage in and inspire students to participate in active resistance against oppression to nurture their engineering and computing identity. It culminates in the final chapter's considerations for creating an integrated, asset-based approach to engineering and computing identity.

SARAH'S TESTIMONIO

As I reflect on my journey into the realm of engineering and computing education and how I embarked on writing a Chicana feminist–informed approach to identity, I am reminded of my own identity as a proud Mexican American woman. This personal connection fuels my vested interest in the communities I write about and aim to serve. Even though I participated in STEM-based courses and activities when I was younger, such as University Interscholastic League (UIL) Calculator Applications and the Texas High School Aerospace

Scholars, I ultimately distanced myself from anything related to STEM. As a young Latina, I did not see people who looked like me in engineering and computing roles. However, destiny had more in store for me than I could fathom, and I would eventually chart a course back to these worlds.

Prior to my PhD studies, I was completely oblivious and painfully ignorant of my Latina identity, history, and culture. My family *never* talked about it, and it was *never* mentioned in my K–12 or higher education learning environments, much to the disappointment of many Texas scholars and activists who I *know* were (and still are) fighting for my right to an ethnic studies education. I might have gone on like this had it not been for the decision to complete the Graduate Portfolio Program in Mexican American Studies (MAS) at the University of Texas at Austin. This experience literally changed my life. I began learning about the painful oppression of my ancestors, and I began rebuilding a sense of culture that had systematically been beaten—literally and physically—out of my *familia* as they were forced to assimilate to white norms and culture. Dr. Nicole M. Guidotti Hernandez taught my first MAS course from an unapologetic Chicana feminist standpoint, uplifting the works of many scholars such as Gloria Anzaldúa, Cherríe Moraga, and Aída Hurtado, and unraveling the history of the Chicano Movement in all of its triumphs and complications.

I carried this experience with me as I shaped my dissertation and early research agenda, but it took almost ten years into my faculty career to fully appreciate how Chicana feminism and a sociohistorically contextualized approach needed to guide the work that I was doing. My dissertation focused on Latina students and STEM identity, with an emphasis on understanding how issues of intersectionality influenced that sense of identity. Although I ultimately used traditional identity models for the dissertation, I wrote way back then about the promise of Chicana feminist approaches as a future direction for the work.

Upon becoming a faculty member, I was quickly swept up into the world of grant-funded STEM initiatives. These collaborations were dedicated to unraveling the field-specific experiences of engineering and computing students. Since the beginning of my career, my work has shifted toward a more nuanced understanding of the engineering and computing identity experiences of Latina students in higher education. Today, my research endeavors revolve around the probing examination of systemic inequities such as racism, sexism, and classism that marginalized communities face as they transition to and navigate through their engineering and computing higher education experiences. My expertise encompasses the utilization of identity and critical frameworks to dissect the formal and informal trajectories of historically marginalized student populations within engineering and computing. This research zeroes in on issues of equity, access, and retention, all intertwined with the complex tapestry of identity, intersectionality, and the overarching systems of oppression that underscore our educational structures.

Of all the STEM areas, I felt like engineering and computing were simultaneously the most problematic and promising areas in which I could focus my work. And although my work has exposed me to a variety of students and contexts, my core concern remains rooted in the experiences of Latina students. This book was an opportunity to honor the quiet voice and writing of my younger self—the emerging Latina scholar calling for a Chicana feminist approach to identity. There is something that feels almost full circle about this journey, a coming home to the work that has been with me for so long.

A GUIDE TO THE UPCOMING CHAPTERS

Chapter 1: The Need for a Chicana Feminist Approach to Engineering and Computing Identity for Latina Students

Chapter 1 explains the urgency of translating what we know into practice and introduces the concept of using Chicana feminism as a lens for equity-minded practitioners to address engineering and computing identity for Latina college students. It outlines the exclusionary nature of engineering and computing, both historically and contemporarily, and provides an overview of the experiences of Latina students within those contexts. It highlights the challenges of these students as well as the assets that they bring with them into the engineering and computing college context.

Chapter 2: Reimagining Engineering and Computing Identity for Latina Students Using a Chicana Feminist Approach

Chapter 2 outlines five guiding principles, inspired by a Chicana feminist approach, for reimagining engineering and computing identity for Latina students. The chapter emphasizes how equity-minded practitioners can use asset-based and sociohistorically situated approaches to view identity as complex, fluid, and dynamic. It also connects practitioners to the idea of reimagining engineering and computing identity for Latina students as a form of resistance.

Chapter 3: Generating Engineering and Computing Identity Recognition

Chapter 3 discusses how equity-minded practitioners can enhance engineering and computing identity recognition by creating support structures that enhance self-recognition and outside recognition for Latina students. The chapter explores how to support self-recognition by enhancing compositional diversity, promoting experiential learning, creating rites of passage, and encouraging cultural heritage and identity. It also explores how to support outside recognition by redefining who is important to outside recognition, expanding opportunities for Latina students to share work and be recognized both on and off campus, and providing opportunities for recognition in engineering and computing internships.

Chapter 4: Supporting Latina Student Engineering and Computing Interests

Chapter 4 examines how equity-minded practitioners can support engineering and computing interests by creating support structures that address both early and continuing interests during college. The chapter examines how to encourage early engineering and computing interests by shaping course offerings, creating educational plans that attend to interest development, and structuring first-year interest groups that center those interests. The chapter also addresses how to nurture engineering and computing interests throughout the degree by investing in digital and physical spaces, facilitating interest-led goal setting, and funding students' travel to identity-based national conferences.

Chapter 5: Building Latina Student Competence and Performance in Engineering and Computing

Chapter 5 outlines how equity-minded practitioners can build student competence and performance for Latina students in engineering and computing. The chapter explores how classrooms can improve by uplifting knowledge cocreation, introducing and scaffolding key concepts and remaining flexible, and integrating the diverse world of engineering and computing surrounding students. In addition, the chapter also details how support services can address help-seeking behaviors and build out tutoring and supplemental instruction, as well as commit to meaningful identity-informed mentoring experiences and develop teaching assistants.

Chapter 6: Creating and Sustaining the Relationships Needed for Developing Engineering and Computing Identity

Chapter 6 explores how equity-minded practitioners can create and sustain the relationships needed to enhance engineering and computing identities of Latina college students. This chapter encourages practitioners to build relationships that amplify engineering and computing interests by supporting Latina students as complex individuals and expanding their competence and performance through relationship building that is dynamic and responsive. The chapter also identifies the need to center identity recognition opportunities by creating relationships that respect history, culture, and Latina ways of knowing.

Chapter 7: Engaging in Resistance to Nurture Engineering and Computing Identity

Chapter 7 encourages equity-minded practitioners to engage in resistance to nurture engineering and computing identity for Latina college students. The chapter outlines four Chicana feminist–inspired strategies to guide how equity-minded practitioners can engage in resistance to nurture engineering and computing identity. It encourages practitioners to reconcile the idea of *nepantla* (explained in chapter 2) with the engineering and computing identity context and make space for reflection and critical consciousness building. It also encourages practitioners to confront issues of whiteness and oppression within these contexts and engage in spiritual activism to transform engineering and computing identity for Latina students.

Chapter 8: Working Together: How Institutions Can Facilitate a Collective, Multipronged Approach to Enhancing Engineering and Computing Identity for Latina Students

Chapter 8 addresses how institutions can facilitate a collective, multipronged approach to enhancing engineering and computing identity for Latina college students. This multipronged approach calls upon practitioners, including faculty, advisors, and support professionals, to work together in these efforts.

APPROACHES TO MAKING THE MOST OF THIS BOOK

In the chapters of this book, I share research-informed concrete strategies, drawing from my own research, for how equity-minded practitioners can support engineering and computing identity practices for Latina students as they progress through their educational journeys. The book challenges practitioners to create equitable, culturally-affirming structures to enhance engineering and computing identity and actively seek out ways to support these endeavors. Practitioners have the capacity to make changes on campuses, within departments, and inside classrooms to ensure that Latina students in engineering and computing see themselves as future engineers and computer scientists.

Throughout the book, I also provide Latina student vignettes and individual and institutional spotlights that further illustrate how equity-minded practitioners might engage or connect with others who are doing this work. The Latina student vignettes represent stories taken directly from participants over the past decade. These vignettes are meant to illuminate issues present among the engineering and computing identity experiences of Latina students and are to be used as illustrative tools for readers. The practitioner showcases highlight individuals, programs, or initiatives that I believe are effective at cultivating engineering and computing identity for Latina students (among other students) in higher education. These spotlights are meant to demonstrate the creativity and dedication of individuals and institutions committed to improving experiences and to create a network of practitioners to share evidence-based approaches. These vignettes and spotlights allow a window into the lives, experiences, challenges, and promising practices that can and do exist around us. They serve to humanize this work and situate it within the communities that we serve and the committed colleagues who exist among us.

I recommend reading and reflecting on this book in community with others and joining together to use this book as a tool to talk through your specific campus context and Latina population to envision new possibilities. And although I do not believe in nor profess to offer a panacea for addressing engineering and computing identity, it is my hope that this book will provide concrete strategies that energize and deepen conversations and take meaningful steps toward action to address white supremacy and other oppressions that threaten this work.

CHAPTER 1

The Need for a Chicana Feminist Approach to Engineering and Computing Identity for Latina Students

May we do work that matters. Vale la pena.

–Gloria Anzaldúa[1]

If you have picked up this book, there is little doubt that you agree with Anzaldúa's sentiment that it is important that we do work that matters. For many of us focused on educational equity, what we do is a life calling, an indescribable desire to better the world around us and to serve our communities and the communities we help create in ways that nourish us both professionally and personally. Doing work that matters requires investing in people and communities and being strong enough to weather both the brilliant moments of shining hope and aliveness that come with doing our job and the darkest moments of disappointment and despair that inevitably also come with it. But, as Anzaldúa reminds us, *vale la pena*, which means that it is worth the pain to do work that matters. Equity-minded practitioners know this all too well. And while you could be doing any number of other things, I am thankful that you have chosen to share in this journey with me as I unpack how we can connect our desire to do work that matters to enhance engineering and computing identity for Latina students.

This chapter discusses the urgency that equity-minded practitioners face in translating what we know into engineering and computing practices. Not a day goes by when I do not read about diversity, equity, and inclusion (DEI) practices coming under scrutiny or being eradicated altogether. The time is now for equity-minded professionals to continue to do the work and, dare I say, make a recommitment to this work to transcend the contemporary obstacles that lie ahead of us. This chapter also provides an important foundation for the rest of the book by outlining why we need a Chicana feminist–informed approach to engineering and computing identity, highlighting the sociohistorical context in which this work rests and the challenges students encounter, as well as the assets that Latina students bring with them on the journey.

ON THE URGENCY OF TRANSLATING WHAT WE KNOW INTO PRACTICE

There is an almost ubiquitous belief that engineering and computing identity is an essential aspect of becoming a part of one's field. An engineering and computing identity includes elements of interest (i.e., desire to learn and curiosity), competence (i.e., knowledge and skills), recognition (i.e., viewing oneself as the kind of person who does engineering or computing and having others view you as this kind of person too), and performance (i.e., social display of knowledge and skills). Engineering and computing identity for Latina women refers to how they understand and position themselves within their field's environment. It illuminates how one associates oneself with or becomes alienated from engineering and computing communities and their norms and cultures.

Although a good body of research on how to enhance engineering and computing identity does exist and will be presented in this book, much of the work that has been completed does not reach the hands of equity-minded practitioners. However, the devil is in the details. We do not often discuss exactly *what* that means in practice or what assumptions, values, and complications exist in doing this work. In so many instances, scholarship stops short of enacting a truly research-to-practice approach, meaning that conceptually, we, as scholars, may have a sense of how to enhance engineering and computing identity for Latina students, but that knowledge is not translated to, or done in tandem with, the practitioners who most need it. As such, the call for change begins with equity-minded practitioners who are willing and capable of being institutional agents dedicated to serving the engineering and computing identity needs of Latina students.[2]

FIGURE 1.1 On the urgency of translating what we know into practice

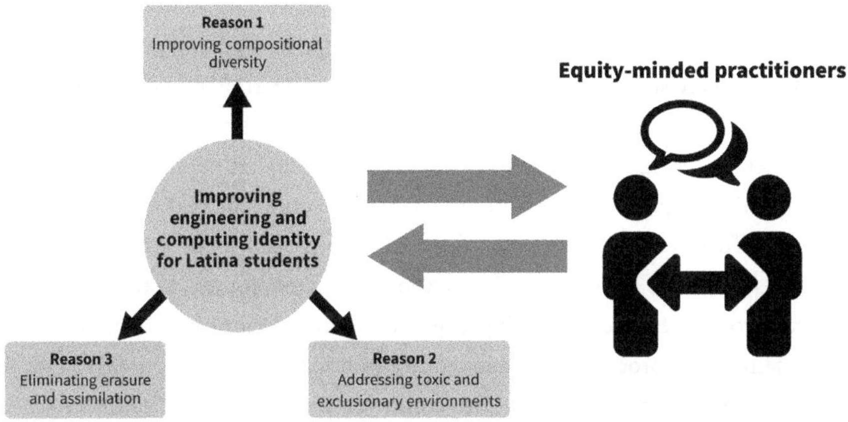

In the following sections (and within figure 1.1), I briefly outline three key reasons why equity-minded practitioners should focus on engineering and computing identity: (1) improving compositional diversity, (2) addressing toxic and exclusionary environments, and (3) eliminating erasure and assimilation.

REASON 1: IMPROVING COMPOSITIONAL DIVERSITY

We urgently need actionable strategies to support Latinas in engineering and computing because of their disparate enrollment, retention, and graduation rates.

Made up of over 62.1 million people, the Latin*[3] community composes 19 percent of the nation's population and is the nation's second largest racial/ethnic group behind white Americans.[4] While the number of bachelor's degrees awarded to Latin* students in engineering and computing has increased over the past decade, the share of Latina women receiving those degrees has increased only slightly over that time.[5] Latinas earned more bachelor's degrees in psychology, social sciences, and biological and agricultural sciences than in engineering and computing, and they attained fewer bachelor's degrees in these fields than white men or women.[6] The fields of engineering and computing may be even more difficult for Latina students to navigate due to their historically exclusionary nature and lack of gender parity. In engineering, Latino men earned 3.5 times the number of bachelor's degrees in engineering as Latina women did, and Latina women earned only 2 percent of all computing bachelor's degrees.[7] Their share of engineering and computing bachelor degree attainment has remained flat (around 2 percent) over the past twenty years despite overall increases in bachelor degree attainment.

Given these statistics, we urgently need actionable strategies to support Latinas in engineering and computing. Because identity is such an integral piece of the engineering and computing experience, focusing on this area provides equity-minded practitioners with a targeted direction for making meaningful change. To improve compositional diversity, we must focus on getting more Latina students to see themselves as engineers and computer scientists. In addition, beyond merely encouraging engineering and computing identity, a Chicana feminist approach encourages equity-minded practitioners to rethink how we grow that compositional diversity and what it means to be a Latina engineer or computer scientist.

REASON 2: ADDRESSING TOXIC AND EXCLUSIONARY ENVIRONMENTS

We urgently need strategies to address the toxic and exclusionary cultures of engineering and computing that Latina students encounter.

Engineering and computing have long been considered toxic and exclusionary learning environments for several reasons, including poor teaching practices, the culture of competition, and high workload, isolation, and pressures experienced by students.[8] Examining the historically and contemporarily exclusionary nature of engineering and computing requires us to have both a clear understanding of what these fields are and a working understanding of the origins of such exclusionary practices. Engineering, at its core, is the intertwining of math and science to solve complex, real-world problems as well as to build, design, and innovate products and processes. The term *engineer* derives from the Latin *ingenium*, meaning "cleverness" and *ingeniare*, "to contrive, devise," according to the *Oxford English Dictionary*.[9] Similarly, *computing*, from the Latin *computāre*, meaning to "calculate, count, or reckon with," is often a space of innovation and exploration that utilizes technological and social understandings to calculate, process, or solve complex problems using both hardware and software.[10]

Engineering programs can be highly competitive, with students vying for top grades or prestigious internships and job offers. This culture of competition can create an environment where students feel pressure to constantly perform, and this pressure often causes students to be reluctant to ask for help or admit when they are struggling. For many engineering students, the heavy workload and persistent barriers to seeking help result in a culture that exacerbates stress and mental health issues.[11] This can create an environment where students are under a great deal of pressure to succeed, which can lead to stress, anxiety, and burnout. Marginalized students, such as Latina students, may also experience discrimination in engineering spaces and feel unwelcome or excluded, which can negatively impact their academic performance and mental health.[12] Students from marginalized groups often experience harassment or discrimination from peers or faculty, which can create a hostile and toxic learning environment.[13]

Similarly, the oppressive nature of computing educational spaces, including a computing culture that thrives on competition, long hours, exploitation, and profits and that can be a hostile place for women, has been well-established.[14] As in engineering, computing students may also encounter a lack of diversity among their peers, faculty, and industry players and may face intense harassment and discrimination from those around them.[15] This environment often leads to students from marginalized groups feeling unwelcome or excluded, which can negatively affect their academic performance and well-being. Stereotypes and biases, both implicit and explicit, can also be pervasive in computing.[16] For example, women may be stereotyped as not being as skilled in computing as men, or racially and ethnically marginalized students may be assumed to be less competent than their white peers. Unfortunately, many Latina computing students face such harassment and discrimination, both inside and outside of the classroom, as they move through their educational careers.[17] Together, these experiences can make it difficult for Latina students to see themselves as engineers or computer scientists and question whether this is the right place for them. What are these environments asking Latina students to endure to transition into the field? How much are they willing to bear before it becomes too much? How much must they compromise their well-being in order to feel a part of this world?

Equity-minded practitioners can address the toxic and exclusionary environments of engineering and computing that Latina students encounter through a concerted effort to acknowledge and act toward practices that forefront identity in ways that are asset based, expansive, and affirming. A Chicana feminist approach can encourage practitioners to (re)construct engineering and computing identity-building experiences that do not force Latina students to conceal pieces of themselves or absorb into an identity that is not authentic to them.

REASON 3: ELIMINATING ERASURE AND ASSIMILATION

We urgently need strategies to address the identity erasure and assimilation of Latina students in engineering and computing.

Prior research has demonstrated that Latina students are not being served equitably; however, serving Latina students in engineering and computing fields is essential to ensuring equity, diversity of thought, and social justice in efforts that lead to persistence in college and later inclusion in the workforce. Engineering and computing have the power to shape the world we live in, and it is important that this power is wielded by a diverse group of people who represent the full spectrum of human experience. Diversity of thought, backgrounds, and experiences among individuals makes the engineering and computing fields a more fruitful place for innovative problem-solving and solutions. Diverse engineering and computing teams bring a variety of perspectives and experiences to the table, which can lead to more innovative and effective solutions to complex problems. By incorporating a range of viewpoints, diverse teams are better equipped to address the diverse needs of the communities they serve. This can lead to more innovative designs and approaches, which can ultimately improve the quality and efficiency of engineering and computing projects.

Even when Latina students enter and stay in engineering and computing, they may be made to fit a mold of what *others* perceive an engineer to be. They may be forced to assimilate into their disciplinary cultures or else risk social ostracization or leave altogether. However, it is not our place to push, pull, and mold Latina students into what *we* think their engineering and computing identities should look like. Latina students have a right to see themselves reflected in their engineering and computing environments and to have their identities validated by members of those communities.

APPROACHING ENGINEERING AND COMPUTING IDENTITY WITH CHICANA FEMINISM

Today's Latina students are diverse and come from many backgrounds, with many different struggles, dreams, and goals. I am asking you—my equity-minded colleagues in this work—to challenge what you think you know about engineering and computing identity and to let a more asset-based, culturally rooted perspective lend a guiding lens to the work we do. We need a shift in how we approach problems and offer possible solutions, recognizing that engineering and computing are not neutral places. This shift will require antiracist, restorative, and critical approaches to addressing systematic oppressions and achieving a collective impact.[18] It is my hope that this shift will help liberate Latina students to bring their authentic selves to engineering and computing spaces and allow practitioners to more fully engage in meaningful ways and hold ourselves, our partners, and our communities responsible for serving Latina students.

The primary charge of this work is to share concrete strategies for how equity-minded practitioners can support engineering and computing identity for Latina students as they progress through their educational journeys. This call to action is articulated around a distinctly Chicana feminist approach to enhancing engineering and computing, including recognition of the multiple borderlands of experience.[19] Whether theirs is a geographic or metaphorical border, Latina students may encounter experiences in which they find themselves *ni de aquí ni de allá* (neither here nor there), torn between the values and norms of engineering and computing spaces and those of their communities.[20] Students at the borderlands may experience a dual feeling of both unity and fragmentation as they navigate the college-going process, leaving many to feel as though they are *neither here nor there*. This book encourages equity-minded practitioners to use a Chicana feminist approach to view identity in a more expansive and complex way, emphasizing the dynamic, shifting, and often messy work of becoming oneself within these fields.

What Is Chicana Feminism?

Chicana feminism emerged in the late 1960s and early 1970s as part of the larger Chicano Movement, which was a political, social, and cultural movement aimed at empowering Mexican Americans.[21] Chicana feminists challenge the ways Chicana women have been historically marginalized and oppressed, both within their communities and in wider society. They address issues of gender, race, class, language, and sexuality, and they seek to create a more inclusive and equitable society for all Chicanas.[22] Chicana feminists argue that traditional forms of feminism, which were often developed by white, middle-class women, do not adequately address the experiences of Chicanas.[23] They seek to create a feminism that is grounded in the experiences of Chicanas and that takes into account the ways in which gender, race, class, language, and sexuality intersect and shape the experiences of Mexican American women. Chicana feminism rejects monolithic thinking and expectations that suggest there is one way to be Latina. And although not all Latina engineering and computing students identify as Chicana (i.e., of Mexican American origin or descent) and Chicana feminism is not without its limitations, this approach is a viable starting point to advance a more inclusive approach to being within those spaces that is expansive and moves toward intersectional thought and practice.[24]

The Case for Chicana Feminism in Engineering and Computing

In recent years, scholars have called for identity-conscious, asset-based approaches to leverage Latin* STEM (science, technology, engineering, and mathematics) students' own *conocimientos*, or ways of knowing, including cultural and familial pedagogics and other assets such as students' curiosity, resilience, and resistant capital.[25] Scholars have also called for addressing inequities for Latinas in STEM by reflecting on systems of oppression, honoring the voices of Latinas, and cocreating systematic sustainable collaborations among institutional actors, students, and communities.[26] This book will draw on Chicana feminist concepts, which consider social-cultural, political, and psychological elements of existence, to investigate how Latina students in engineering and computing shape their own identities and can be sites of resistance to oppression (e.g., racism, sexism, colonial domination). This approach underscores the multidimensional identities these students hold, which often position them at the crossroads between their Latin* cultures and the oppressive American educational system. At its core, Chicana feminism can be a radical approach to serving Latina engineering and computing students. We must acknowledge Latina students as having multidimensional identities that often position them at the "borderlands" between their Latin* cultures and the US educational system. This means acknowledging that Latina engineering and computing students have historically and contemporarily existed in a state of marginalization in the US educational system and in US society writ large.

Central to this philosophy is the profound belief that Latina students are not merely recipients of knowledge, but *holders and creators* of knowledge. Latina students inherently and through their engineering and computing experiences gain and expand what we know about the world. Their perspectives are not only valid but also a valuable piece of our existence. Relatedly, Latina students are also creators of knowledge, capable of expanding what we and our communities know about given disciplinary subjects as well as knowledge of what it is like to navigate our world from their standpoint. Through this lens, this book seeks to foster understanding, empathy, and actionable transformation, equipping educators, practitioners, and scholars with the tools to embrace a Chicana feminist approach in nurturing engineering and computing identities among Latina students.

Latina Students in Engineering and Computing: Challenges and Assets

This section outlines the current research on Latina students in engineering and computing, including an understanding of both the challenges and assets that are present within those experiences. Many of the challenges that Latina students face in these fields ultimately make it difficult for them to see themselves in engineering or computing roles. Persistent marginalization and forms of discrimination, both blatant and subtle, can complicate how Latina students build and maintain their identities. However, Latina students in both of these fields have access to a wealth of assets from their families and communities that make it possible not only to be retained but also to embody a more fulfilling engineering or computing identity and career.

Identity Challenges. Research shows that having a strong engineering identity is crucial for the success of students who are traditionally marginalized within an engineering context, and intentional cultivation of Latin* students' engineering identity is key to building strong engineers.[27] Latin* students build their engineering identities from a variety of experiences and sources, including their families and communities, precollege and college experiences, institutions, and personal characteristics.[28] In addition, Latin* engineering students hold a variety of identities and backgrounds, including differences based on gender, sexuality, class, language, phenotype, or nation of origin, which can complicate engineering identity due to existing oppressions and marginalization.[29]

Engineering and computing contexts may be particularly difficult to navigate due to their environments being entrenched in exclusionary, masculine, competitive, and identity-evasive practices.[30] These inequities are the result of historically racist, sexist, and other oppressive structures embedded in STEM.[31]

Historically and contemporarily, women of color in STEM experience a "double bind": they are simultaneously marginalized as women and as people of color within predominantly white men's spaces.[32] Racism and sexism (and other oppressive forces) are perpetuated by formal systems of rules and policies, cultural norms, and personal interactions shaped by those forces.[33] A growing body of literature has demonstrated that women of color in engineering tend to rate their skills and abilities lower than their white women and men counterparts, often experience microaggressions, and may require targeted supports to address challenges associated with intersectionality.[34] *Intersectionality* refers to the presence of multiple intersecting, interlocking identities within an individual that are often connected to multiple forms of oppression.[35] Similarly, a robust body of scholarship has articulated the nature of isolationist, racist, and sexist contexts for women of color in computing and has called for culturally relevant pedagogical approaches and theory to address the negative experiences these contexts produce.[36] Because such oppressive structures are inescapable, to persist toward degree completion in engineering and computing, Latina students must operate within systems of oppression, with success often dependent upon their navigation skills.[37]

Specifically, research on Latina students in engineering has highlighted the lack of diversity and meaningful faculty interaction and the rigid grading policies Latina students experience at the department level, as well as the threats to their sense of belonging in predominantly masculine programs.[38] My research has demonstrated that families are a positive influence on engineering identity for Latina students, often leading students to engineering in the first place or providing a source of motivation to be successful and pay it forward.[39] In addition, we found that women and Latin* identity-based STEM organizations encouraged strong engineering identity. We also found that intersecting identities, such as immigrant student status, race/ethnicity, gender, and motherhood, influence engineering identity.

Similarly, Latin* computing students in higher education may face a series of challenges related to underrepresentation, discrimination, sense of belonging, and cultural expectations and perspectives. Although the Latin* student population continues to grow on college campuses, that representation is not reflected in an increase in diversity within computing.[40] As a result, Latin* students continue to face racism and discrimination (e.g., lack of access to resources and opportunities, language marginalization inside and outside of the classroom) as well as a lack of sense of belonging and feelings of isolation that can influence their computing engagement.[41] Latin* computing students may also experience a clash of cultural and familial expectations and obligations, which can influence their ability to fully participate in computing programs.[42] Latin* students may also experience conflicting perspectives on the purpose and value of computing education and seek out computing careers that have a social or community focus.[43]

Together, these experiences may pose challenges to building and maintaining an engineering or computing identity that is authentic to them as Latina students. And although Latina students might be resilient enough to overcome these challenges, it is the responsibility of practitioners to question and act on why these challenges exist in the first place. Rather than placing obstacles in the identity-building process of Latina engineering and computing students, equity-minded practitioners might seek remove those obstacles and consider how they might also leverage the rich assets that these students bring to the educational process.

The Assets. Although they may experience challenges, Latina students also bring a wealth of home- and community-based assets (e.g., supportive friends and family) to their journeys, which informs their engineering and computing identities.[44] Latina women utilize myriad forms of community cultural wealth (CCW) to navigate challenges within engineering and computing.[45] CCW, whose roots lie in critical race theory, acknowledges the various forms of wealth that students use, in this case, to navigate educational systems and disrupt oppressive cultures. Students use familial capital (e.g., emotional, content knowledge) as a bridge to knowledge and sources of support; navigational capital (e.g., navigation strategies shared by peers, TRiO office support) to maneuver in computing and engineering fields; and resistant capital (e.g., outreach, critiquing the field) to challenge marginalization and sexism in these fields. Latina students in computing often draw on both individual experiences and the world around them when constructing their engineering and computing identities.[46] Students are influenced not only by daily sense-making regarding their precollege and college-going experiences but also by community cultural wealth and funds of identity.[47] Community cultural wealth and funds of identity recognize the social and cultural capital that Latina students can draw on from their families and communities to use toward success in engineering and computing. Latina students often feel a sense of uncertainty about their place in engineering and computing and go to peers, student groups, family, professional conferences, and faculty connections to overcome adversity on their journeys.[48] Latina students often actively resist marginalization by acknowledging their journeys as trailblazers and engaging with identity-based STEM organizations that affirm and uplift them.[49] Latina students also engage in acts of internal and external transformational resistance, including community transformation and healing, and in challenging inequitable environments in their fields.[50]

All of these assets not only empower Latina students to navigate often oppressive engineering and computing spaces but also validate and sustain these students on their road to building and maintaining identity. When leveraged correctly, equity-minded practitioners can encourage students to draw upon these assets as they consider the kind of engineer or computer scientist that they want to become. However, simply because students hold these assets does not automatically mean that institutions, and the individuals associated with those institutions, will immediately value and support these various assets. It is the responsibility of equity-minded practitioners to ensure that the assets that Latina students bring with them are recognized as valuable and important to the identity journey.

CONCLUSION

Throughout this book, I continue to draw on Chicana feminism and engage these critical concepts in ways that will support your work. In the chapters ahead, I outline how a Chicana feminist approach to identity for Latina students can ultimately create a better experience for these students. Beginning with chapter 2's commitment to reimagining engineering and computing identity and throughout the book's middle chapters, which address the strategies for enhancing support structures, relationships, and resistance, I bring you toward an understanding of how we might use the Chicana feminist guiding principles to create support structures for meaningful change in identity practices. In the book's final chapters, I encourage you to push boundaries a bit as we think about ways to encourage and engage in acts of resistance and create a multipronged approach to enhancing engineering and computing identity for Latina students.

CHAPTER 2

Reimagining Engineering and Computing Identity for Latina Students Using a Chicana Feminist Approach

To reimagine identity in new ways requires that we change the focus of the lens trained on our faces and shift our perceptions.

–Gloria Anzaldúa[1]

If we are to reimagine engineering and computing identity for Latina students, we must, as Gloria Anzaldúa urges, recontextualize, reinterpret, and recreate our thinking around this issue. Rather than stay bound to the same approaches, we are compelled, by our responsibility to students and our commitment to higher education, to shift our ways of thinking and seeing. We must "change the focus of the lens" to fully transform our own perceptions, positions, and directions to ensure that our Latina students can assume engineering and computing identities.

Over the past few decades, we have seen substantial gains in the number of Latina students entering and persisting in careers in engineering and computing. And in many ways, we stand on the shoulders of giants—trailblazers who have come before us—lighting and forging engineering and computing pathways that were the wildest dreams of our ancestors. However, much of our history within these fields has been focused on enhancing compositional diversity and assimilating to the dominant white and masculine cultures of engineering and computing. Within this model, Latina students cannot bring their full selves to their work and build authentic engineering and computing identities. We must move beyond traditional methods to embrace a world in which Latina students are supported and empowered to be the authors and experts of their own experiences. The overarching message of this chapter is that if we are to retain their talents in engineering and computing contexts, we must understand that Latina students and their knowledge matter. Their multiple identities, complex histories, and assets must be honored and incorporated into the work that we do to shape engineering and computing identity.

This chapter outlines **five guiding principles** (outlined in figure 2.1), inspired by a Chicana feminist approach, for reimagining engineering and computing identity for Latina students. This conceptual chapter encourages equity-minded practitioners to take an asset-based and sociohistorically situated

FIGURE 2.1 Overview of the five guiding principles

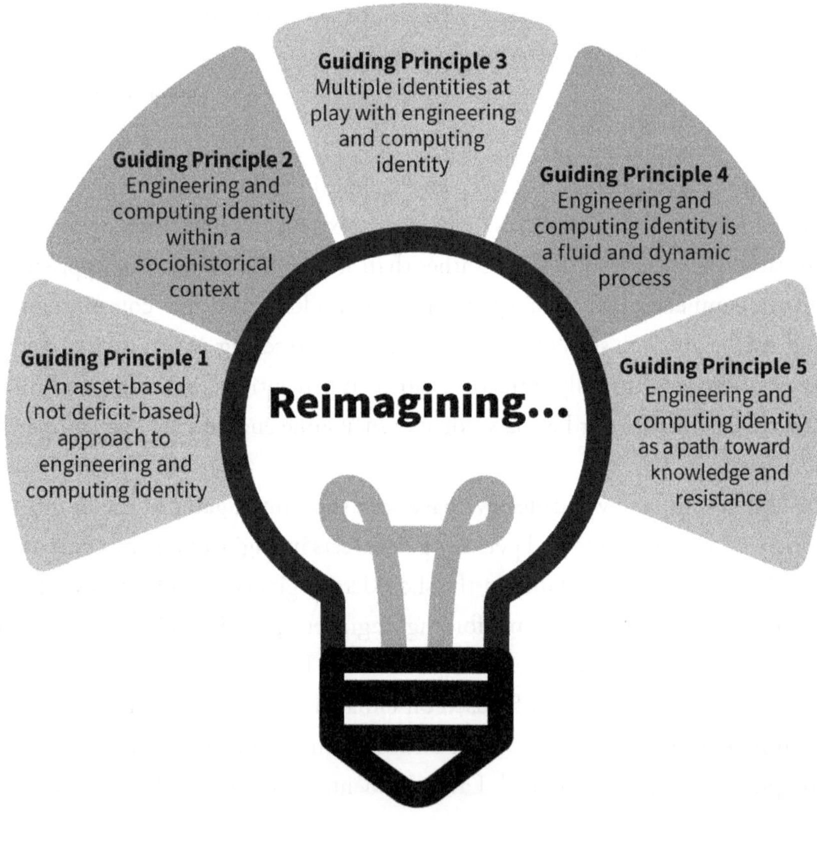

approach to engineering and computing identity that recognizes Latina students as holders and creators of knowledge who have agency. These guiding principles also emphasize the range of identities that Latina students possess, which may become more or less salient during their dynamic identity journey. Finally, these guiding principles support a culture of deep reflection and point toward engineering and computing identity as a path toward *conocimiento* (knowledge) and resistance to white, masculine norms and values that threaten to push Latina students out of these fields. Multigenerational white norms and values present in the engineering and computing fields, such as perfectionism, individualism, and monistic thinking, coupled with masculine norms and values, such as toughness and antifemininity or status and competition, create a hostile learning environment in which Latina students must either assimilate, resist, or be pushed out. As such, equity-minded practitioners must remove barriers and encourage Latina students to resist stereotypes and ways of knowing and being that seek to overlook them as engineers and computer scientists. Practitioners should also strive to counter deficit thinking that paints Latina students and their communities as somehow broken and in need of "fixing."

This chapter outlines the guiding principles of a Chicana-informed approach to engineering and computing identity for Latina students. Subsequent chapters will provide examples illustrating ways to put these principles into action. These guiding principles represent what I believe to be the most important elements of Chicana feminism that can help equity-minded practitioners guide the work. Is there more to Chicana feminism than just these five principles? Absolutely. Chicana feminism is a deeply complex theorizing space to which scholars and practitioners from around the world have contributed over the years. There are many layers of understanding and nuance that cannot possibly fit within these pages. As such, this chapter represents my attempt to distill this approach down to five guiding principles that are accessible ways to start the conversation and provide a pathway toward growing knowledge and resistance.

GUIDING PRINCIPLE 1: AN ASSET-BASED (NOT DEFICIT-BASED) APPROACH TO ENGINEERING AND COMPUTING IDENTITY

The first guiding principle emphasizes that practitioners should utilize an **asset-based approach** that acknowledges that Latina students are not merely recipients of knowledge but are **holders and creators of knowledge who have**

agency to shape their own engineering and computing identities and transform their societies.

Two schools of thought generally undergird approaches to engineering and computing identity: those that are deficit based and those that are asset based. A deficit standpoint is one in which practitioners may view students as being inherently flawed or lacking in a variety of ways, often attributing such flaws to their backgrounds or intersecting identities.[2] Taking a deficit-based approach ignores the rich histories, cultures, and ways of knowing that inherently come from Latin* families and communities. Deficit-based approaches to engineering and computing identity often focus on "fixing" students or shaping them into what they consider the ideal engineer or computer scientist, without regard to students' individual needs or sense of agency or self. These "ideal" models are often steeped in white supremacy and masculine norms and limit possibilities for how Latina students could define engineering and computing for themselves. Practices employing a deficit-based approach to engineering and computing identity can often leave students feeling as though they are the ones who lack sufficient knowledge, skills, or experiences or that they must assimilate to fit the mold of a specific kind of engineer or computer scientist. Denying students the ability to focus on their needs, agency, or sense of self is at best paternalistic and at worst dehumanizing. Correspondingly, a deficit-based approach often does not acknowledge the systemic, intersecting oppressions such as racism and sexism, described in chapter 1, that Latina students often face, nor does it work toward dismantling those systems of oppression. Deficit-based approaches maintain the status quo and force Latina students to erase or assimilate parts of their identity. Many practitioners, even those who are well-intentioned, may approach supporting students from a deficit standpoint.

In contrast, asset-based approaches see inherent value in the student and celebrate their individual and group qualities, characteristics, and ways of knowing. Such approaches focus on the strengths that Latina students bring with them from their families and communities into the college setting. Rather than viewing Latina students as individuals or a group in need of "fixing," asset-based approaches address how practitioners can examine and tailor learning environments to ensure student success and create conditions that enhance engineering and computing identity. Relatedly, an asset-based approach to identity calls upon equity-minded practitioners to value the cultural backgrounds, funds of identity, and community cultural wealth that students bring with them.[3] Practitioners should take action to support engineering and computing identities by acknowledging and leveraging the aspirational, linguistic, familial, navigational, social, and resistant capital that students possess.[4] Put plainly, equity-minded practitioners should find ways for students to leverage familial and social capital by increasing student social connections and integrating diverse ways of knowing as well as creating outlets to allow students to build resistant capital by addressing stereotypes and white norms and values in constructive ways, such as engaging in feedback loops with practitioners.

Ideally, asset-based approaches to engineering and computing identity should strive to encourage Latina students to live and shape their identities authentically and unapologetically, rather than make them feel bound by assimilationist notions of what it means to be an engineer or computer scientist. Engineering and computing contexts often force Latina students to adhere to white, masculine norms or suffer isolation and marginalization. However, it is the responsibility of equity-minded practitioners to ensure that Latina students can bring their whole selves to these contexts.

To live authentically and unapologetically might mean that Latina students do not have to apologize for their backgrounds, perceived shortcomings, or cultural values and that they can feel a sense of empowerment to engage with their full identities without regret or risk of social ostracization or isolation. Asset-based approaches, at their core, should honor and uplift the voices, perspectives, and storytelling of Latina engineering and computing students to push toward liberation and the transformation of their academic spaces. Practically, this might mean featuring Latina students in departmental magazines, websites, or social media. It could also look like incorporating Latina professional engineers and computer scientists into events or partnerships to share their stories and the assets that they brought with them. Doing so allows for other Latina students, both peers and coming generations, to see the value in embodying engineering and computing identities that are authentic to themselves.

GUIDING PRINCIPLE 2: ENGINEERING AND COMPUTING IDENTITY WITHIN A SOCIOHISTORICAL CONTEXT

The second guiding principle emphasizes the need for practitioners to contextualize engineering and computing identity within a sociohistorical context. In

Light in the Dark/Luz en lo Oscuro: Rewriting Identity, Spirituality, Reality, Gloria Anzaldúa emphasizes the importance of understanding sociohistorical contexts and the relationship that individuals have with both the past and the present as they construct their identities: "Who and what we are depends on those surrounding us, a mix of our interactions with our *alrededores*/environments, with new and old narratives. Identity is multilayered, stretching in all directions, from past to present, vertically and horizontally, chronologically and spatially."[5]

Anzaldúa highlights the importance of environments and narratives across time and how those elements influence who we become. Practitioners should contextualize engineering and computing identity for Latina students within appropriate historical and contemporary **sociohistorical contexts**. Contextualizing identity in this way not only empowers Latina student to know and be connected to their history and surroundings but also validates them and Latin* communities as holders and creators of knowledge and resistance in ways that students may not have been exposed to before.

The foundation of this guiding principle is the belief that individuals cannot be disentangled from the contexts within which they live and are educated and that it is impossible to separate the individual and their identity from larger historical and societal contexts. Recognizing this can inform our understanding of how various contexts have shaped the collective narratives and individual stories of Latina students as they progress toward becoming engineers or computer scientists and can give practitioners touchstones from which to build a more robust understanding of the student experience.

Practitioners should situate educational initiatives and support services within the social and historical contexts in which Latina engineering and computing students have found themselves both in the past and currently. Doing so requires that we attend to the past histories of Latin* communities, including histories of their countries of origin, colonization, and migration patterns. This can be important for serving first-generation as well as continuing-generation Latina students in these fields, who may experience a range of identity needs.

It also means attending to the living history and present social contexts of varied Latinx communities, including cultural norms and values and current events that influence engineering and computing identity. Understanding cultural norms and values (e.g., *familismo*, spirituality, gender expectations) can enhance how practitioners approach engineering and computing identity and involve Latin* communities. Contextualizing engineering and computing identity within local, national, and global current issues can demonstrate to students and communities that educational institutions are responsive to students' needs and committed to their success. Attending to sociohistorical contexts, both past and present, honors the long histories existing within Latinx communities and acknowledges the fact that Latina students may continue to face oppressions such as racism, sexism, classism, and other challenges as a result of engineering and computing learning environments.

Finally, contextualizing work within sociohistorical contexts does not merely mean saying the words or presenting the history, but rather *really* attending to it in meaningful ways that positively influence engineering and computing identity. In many instances, this may mean that practitioners need to learn from students, faculty, staff, and community members within these cultures as well as go on their own journeys by using available resources to more fully understand Latin* communities. From these understandings, practitioners may not only be able to more clearly articulate approaches that attend to these sociohistorical contexts but also become more empathetic and purposeful in how they shape engineering and computing identity experiences for Latina students.

GUIDING PRINCIPLE 3: MULTIPLE IDENTITIES AT PLAY WITH ENGINEERING AND COMPUTING IDENTITY

The third guiding principle highlights the importance of multiple identities for engineering and computing identity. One of the most important concepts one might take from Chicana feminism is the idea that there are multiple and intersecting identities that influence the engineering and computing identity experiences of Latina students. As the scholar Aída Hurtado states, rather than simplifying or essentializing the experiences of Latinas, "Chicana feminists believe in a 'theory of the flesh' that takes into account lived experience in all its complexity."[6] Coined by Cherríe Moraga in *This Bridge Called My Back*, "theory of the flesh" refers to the need for equity-minded practitioners to validate the lived experiences of Latina students in engineering and computing and acknowledges how those lived experiences are the result of physical and racial embodiments. This means that the body, spaces, and experiences that Latina students occupy and undergo are essential to understanding their identity journeys and subsequent efforts to enhance identity. It stresses the contextual nature of identity and points to the need for deep self-reflection and actions toward understanding and counteracting oppression. This may be particularly helpful when thinking of the complexities that make up a Latina student's journey toward an engineering and computing identity as one not just of the mind but also of the body and spirit.

Chicana feminists such as Anzaldúa also emphasize the importance of these identities and of understanding a "geography" of the self by which individuals arrange and rearrange multiple facets of their identities to exist within many worlds:

> It's not really a search for identity because we haven't really lost an identity. Instead, we're figuring out how to arrange, *componer*, all these facets of identity: class and race and belonging to so many worlds—the Chicano world, the academic world, the white world, the world of the job . . . identity is an arrangement or series of clusters, a kind of stacking or layering of selves, horizontal and vertical layers, the geography of selves made up of the different communities you inhabit.[7]

Latina students create and refine a "geography of selves" based on the interactions and experiences that they have within engineering and computing and within their larger communities. Practitioners should acknowledge that Latina engineering and computing students possess **a range of identities** (e.g., gender, race, class, sexuality, generational status) **that become more or less salient** depending on a variety of factors, including environments and systemic, intersectional oppressions.

Latina students in engineering and computing often exist within multiple constituencies and, therefore, have complex identity experiences and needs to which practitioners must attend. Practitioners must acknowledge that these multiple identities cannot be divorced or unlocked from each other. Rather than asking Latina students to identify with a single category, practitioners should acknowledge that it is the intersections of these identities that make and refine identity: "These identity categories—categories based primarily on history, biology, nationality—are important aspects of personal and collective identity; however, they don't contain our entirety, and we can't base our whole *identidad* on them. It's not 'race,' gender, class, or any single attribute but the interaction of all of these aspects (as well as others) that creates identity."[8] Here, Anzaldúa emphasizes not only the importance of multiple identities but also the interactions of various identities as crucial to the process of becoming who we are.

Rather than restrict our efforts to a single category, equity-minded practitioners must be ready and willing to do the complex work of attending to identity. Engineering and computing identity can be both perplexing and challenging for students, particularly as they grapple to make sense of their own multiple identities in spaces that are often unwelcoming to nondominant identities. As such, practitioners should work toward embracing the unique individuality that each Latina student brings. While Anzaldúa emphasizes the multiplicity of identity, she also emphasizes the responsive nature of identity as interactions and changes happen within the individual: "It's supposed to be one. You know, you're one entity—one person with one identity. But that's not so. There are many personalities and subpersonalities in you, and your identity shifts every time you shift positions."[9] Taking a Chicana feminist approach here also looks like observing the importance of salience, or that some identities become more foregrounded depending on where the student is physically, emotionally, psychologically, or spiritually, as well as on what identities may be recognized or marginalized within their environments.

Each Latina student within engineering or computing is on her own personal identity journey and cannot be expected to follow a "traditional" trajectory or pattern of salience regarding any of her identities. Some students may feel that their gender is the most salient identity for them, while others believe that race or ethnicity is the most salient, or in other cases, several identities may coalesce to create unique experiences and challenges. Relatedly, because Latina engineering and computing students respond to the influences of their environments, they may adjust to the oppressions that surround them in ways that either obscure or illuminate their identities and in ways that are sometimes conscious and at other times unconscious. For example, a Latina student at a Hispanic-serving institution (HSI) with a significant Latin* population may feel her race or ethnicity is less important because she is often surrounded by individuals who look like her or speak her language. In engineering and computing spaces, she may become much more aware of her gender because there are fewer Latina women in her classes or student organizations. Likewise, Latina students may feel that their socioeconomic status or gender are much more salient in certain circumstances where they experience nondominant identities. This guiding principle points to the express need of Latina students in engineering and computing to self-determine and become authors and authorities of their own experiences.

From this foundation, equity-minded practitioners can work toward ensuring that student supports, relationship-building, and resistance efforts enable students to draw upon their multiple, intersecting identities.

GUIDING PRINCIPLE 4: ENGINEERING AND COMPUTING IDENTITY IS A FLUID AND DYNAMIC PROCESS

Related to the third guiding principle, the fourth principle centers on the Chicana feminist–inspired concept that engineering and computing identity is a **fluid and continuously evolving process** for Latina students. Engineering and computing identity involves a highly dynamic process of self-discovery and becoming in which there are no clear borders or ways in which to separate identities. Anzaldúa reminds us that identity is marked by transition and change: "Nothing is fixed. The pulse of existence, the heart of the universe, is fluid. Identity, like a river, is always changing, always in transition, always in *nepantla* [in-between space]." *Nepantla* is a term used in Chicana feminism that refers to the in-between space that Latina students in engineering and computing may experience. That in-between space can be a literal or metaphorical space. Latina students may have to literally physically cross between countries, or they may experience a more metaphorical crossing in which they enter a culture like that of engineering or computing, that contrasts with the culture of their home or community. We will continue to explore the concept of this in-betweenness as an important space and experience in the process of *conocimiento*, described later in this chapter and referred to throughout the book.

Anzaldúa admonishes us that "like the river downstream, you're not the same person you were upstream. You begin to define yourself in terms of who you are becoming, not who you have been."[10] Identity is not only fluid but also marked by shifts over time. For our students, identity moves in many directions, often leaving them in spaces of *nepantla* in which they are living at the borders between various identities while becoming engineers or computer scientists. Latina students' identities are constantly moving and responding to outward situations and interactions as well as to how they make sense of engineering and computing experiences. From an Anzaldúan perspective, identity is relational and situated within the interactions between individuals' communities and worlds: "Identity, as consciously and unconsciously created, is always in motion—self interacting with different communities and worlds. Identity is relational."[11] Practitioners must, therefore, acknowledge that an engineering and computing identity requires students to continuously make sense of their encounters and situate their identities within their academic and social environments. Every day, Latina students evaluate encounters with their coursework, peers, faculty members, and advisors, whether consciously or unconsciously. These encounters lead their identity to morph and either move students closer to or further away from a sense of identity.

This contextualization results in engineering and computing identities that continuously evolve, starting from students' early years and continuing across their college years and into the workforce. For example, a Latina student at a community college takes an introductory computing course as an elective and realizes that she is not only interested in the content but also performs well and is recognized by her peers. However, after transfer to another college, that sense of recognition wanes as she struggles in her middle-year courses and gets relegated to group secretarial work (taking notes for her peers) rather than technical work, and she weighs whether she should switch majors. But she stays with it. Her computing identity begins to grow again as she undertakes internships, becomes a teaching assistant for coding classes, and gets involved with the women in computing organization. Her identity reaches a new high when she assumes her first computing industry position.

Thus, engineering and computing identities are not settled or fixed but rather change gradually and are refined over time. We are reminded within Chicana feminism that "identity is an ongoing story, one that changes with each telling, one we revise at each way station, each stop, in our viaje de la vida [life's journey]."[12] Engineering and computing identity experiences are expansive and span one's entire life journey. Therefore, practitioners must reimagine each stage of the educational journey as a potential site of engineering and computing identity. Prior to college, Latina students may wonder what major or program they will pursue or how they can build their skills; after enrollment, they may weigh the costs and benefits of being in their discipline and evaluate whether they feel a sense of belonging to their field. Finally, as they move toward graduation and the workforce, they may weigh whether these fields are, indeed, for them and whether they see themselves engaging in this kind of work long term.

Relatedly, because identity is unique to each student, we must remain flexible and open at each stage of the educational journey to enable Latina students who may be experiencing different "way stations" at different times. Put plainly, practitioners cannot assume a monolithic engineering or computing identity experience, or even a linear or sequential approach to these elements. Instead, practitioners must grapple with the messiness and fluidity that is the engineering and computing identity for Latina students in college. In addition, because Latina students are holders and creators of knowledge, they have a right to practices created by equity-minded practitioners that are flexible and grow with them throughout their engineering and computing journeys.

GUIDING PRINCIPLE 5: ENGINEERING AND COMPUTING IDENTITY AS A PATH TOWARD KNOWLEDGE AND RESISTANCE

The fifth and final guiding principle asserts that practitioners should support a culture of reflection **toward the path of *conocimiento* and resistance**, both for Latina engineering and computing students and for equity-minded practitioners engaged in this work. Anzaldúa emphasizes the role that individuals have in deprogramming themselves as they move toward the *camino de conocimiento* (path of knowledge): "Tu camino de conocimiento requires that you encounter your shadow side and confront what you've programmed yourself (and have been programmed by your cultures) to avoid (desconocer), to confront the traits and habits distorting how you see reality and inhibiting the full use of your facultades."[13]

The *camino de conocimiento* refers to a seven-stage process of consciousness building in which individuals come to deepen their understandings of themselves and process their experiences with a given environment. Understanding Anzaldúa's writing about *conocimiento* can enable equity-minded practitioners to more fully understand how Latina students in engineering and computing navigate the cultures of their fields and their home communities.

The stages of *conocimiento* as applied to engineering and computing identity can include the following:

1. ***Arrebato*:** Referring to rupture or shattering, both a beginning and end, this stage is usually triggered by an important life event or series of situations that may cause Latina students to question their engineering or computing identity and place within these fields. It usually causes a significant disruption and reconsideration of one's identity and pathways.

2. ***Nepantla*:** An in-between space, this stage is often where students feel torn between the cultures of engineering and computing and their Latin* home and communities. Students in this stage are in a state of conflict and often experience their values and beliefs being challenged. An important element of this stage is moving from pain and hopelessness to new understandings and ways of being within engineering and computing.
3. **Coatlicue state:** Coatlicue refers to the powerful Aztec goddess who is considered an earth-mother figure. During this phase, Latina students may become increasingly aware of oppressive forces existing within engineering and computing fields. This stage, often marked by despair, is concerned with how students process oppression and give way to new versions of themselves. It is a space of self-reflection and search for understanding.
4. ***El Compromiso*:** In this call-to-action stage, Latina students must let go of certain parts of themselves that no longer fit or are no longer comfortable. Students emerge from this stage with a deeper understanding of their engineering or computing identity and how they occupy space within these fields and the greater world around them. This stage is all about Latina students reconciling what they know about themselves and their engineering and computing realities with their new selves.
5. **Coyolxauhqui:** Coyolxauhqui refers to an Aztec goddess often connected to the process of ongoing healing from events or experiences. As such, this stage refers to how Latina students reassemble their identities based on their interpretations of the experiences that they have with engineering and computing. It is during this stage that students may heal and reframe who they are as engineers or computer scientists, including how they position themselves within those spaces.
6. **The blow-up:** This stage is a clash of realities in which Latina students in engineering and computing challenge previously held ideas and move into a critique of oppressive forces that have influenced their experiences. Done individually and sometimes within the community, this stage can highlight the stark contrasts that exist for a student's previous engineering or computing identity and their newly reassembled one. This stage is essential to get to the next stage of shifting realities.
7. **Shifting realities:** The last stage of coming to *conocimiento* sees Latina students fully transform their realities and identities as well as push for social

change within engineering and computing spaces. This stage represents the individual act of transforming one's identity through the process of *conocimiento* as well as the more public act of resisting against marginalization of one's identities and experiences.

These stages are not linear in nature and may occur in cycles in which Latina students work through elements of their engineering and computing identities to progress toward a higher stage of consciousness and understanding of one's identity and place within the field.

To facilitate this movement toward a path of knowledge and consciousness, equity-minded practitioners should examine the customs, norms, and ways in which we approach learning experiences for Latina engineering and computing students. In juxtaposition to the fast-paced nature of this world of instant gratification, practitioners must make room for reflection and contemplation of identity. They must allow students the space, time, and energy to engage in forms of reflection in which they can process what is going on in their engineering and computing experiences and gain the agency to make changes accordingly. It is from these sites of reflection that Latina engineering and computing students can find a path to *conocimiento* (path to knowledge) on which they can, more consciously, shape their own identities and engage in resistance against white cultural norms and values. Moving toward resistance looks like empowering Latina students so that they can become the kinds of engineers and computer scientists that they wish to become.

Equity-minded practitioners should acknowledge that this kind of work takes time, reflection, and a reshaping and reimaging of our worldview of what it means to build and maintain an engineering or computing identity. Similarly, practitioners must also recognize that *conocimiento*, the path to knowing and understanding, is not just an intellectual one, but one of the mind, body, and spirit that requires supporting Latina students to gain an awareness of the current structures and injustices within engineering and computing as well as building capacity and commitment to address those injustices. On an individual level, this consciousness can help Latina students within engineering and computing make sense of and have the language to articulate previous and current educational experiences. Especially if those experiences have been laden with trauma or if a student is struggling with her engineering or computing identity, individual-level consciousness-building can be healing and build resilience. At a systemic level, consciousness-building is the foundation for encouraging Latina students to critique and advocate for changing engineering and computing structures alongside similarly minded peers and mentors.

Finally, inherent within this guiding principle is the incredibly important **role of equity-minded practitioners engaging in their own path toward knowledge and resistance.** Similar to the actions practitioners take to create environments that support Latina students to authentically refine their engineering and computing identity, practitioners must also be on such a journey. Practitioners must confront their own ignorance, their own prejudices, and their own assumptions, and they must reflect on how *they* might engage in their own forms of resistance that press toward a greater sense of connectedness and relatedness for engineering and computing identity. This might mean admitting that you, even as an equity-minded practitioner, do not exist on an island or in a vacuum and are on your own journey to consciousness. Chicana feminism, at a foundational level, encourages us to know ourselves and move toward understanding those around us to build a true sense of identity and community.

CONCLUSION

The work that I have done over the past decade and these guiding principles serve as a conceptual foundation for the latter part of the book, which provides recommendations for creating the supports, building and sustaining the necessary relationships, and engaging in resistance to support engineering and computing identity for Latina students. If we do not reimagine engineering and computing identity, the foundation upon which we build our initiatives and where we choose to invest time, money, and energy will suffer, and ultimately, we will fail to make sustainable change. If we fail to consider these guiding principles as we shape identity experiences, we will fail to realize the full potential of our relationship-building and relationship-sustaining efforts, particularly those deeply rooted in a shared sense of trust, transparency, mutuality, and connectedness. And if we push out Latinas from engineering and computing contexts, we risk losing their talent in our American workforce and further marginalizing a rapidly growing community within our nation.

At their core, these guiding principles not only represent a commitment to supporting engineering and computing identity but also, perhaps more importantly, a path toward *conocimiento* (knowledge) and resistance against white, masculine values and norms so that Latina students can authentically bring themselves to these spaces. It is my hope that practitioners will approach this work from an asset-based standpoint grounded in reimagining what we can do differently, how we can change the system, and how we can support and serve students in both individual and collective terms.

CHAPTER 3

Generating Engineering and Computing Identity Recognition

Qué hacer de aquí y cómo?. . . Caminante, no hay puentes, se hace puentes al andar.

[What to do from here and how?. . . Trailblazer, border-crosser, there are no bridges, one builds them as one walks.]

–Gloria Anzaldúa[1]

The previous chapter outlined five guiding principles inspired by Chicana feminism that can inspire you to reimagine engineering and computing identity for Latina students. Yet this begs the question: Where do we go from here? How do we, as equity-minded practitioners, create Chicana feminist–informed support structures for engineering and computing identity? In just a few short words, Gloria Anzaldúa's writings not only guide practitioners to ask these questions but also provide answers for moving forward. Anzaldúa reminds us, as *caminantes* (trailblazers, border-crossers), that it is *we* who build the bridges as we journey ahead. Within this quote, Anzaldúa addresses her audience as *caminantes,* from the word *caminar* (to walk), which denotes a type of wayfarer or foot traveler with a purpose or destination in mind, perhaps even invoking images of *caminantes* who make spiritual journeys. As Anzaldúa suggests, *caminantes* explore spaces and contexts where there may be little structure in the direction that we would like to move in. But we, nevertheless, must continue forward, building those structures as we go. Equity-minded practitioners are the *caminantes* who build the bridges, blaze the trails, and move us forward.

Over the next three chapters (chapters 3–5), I outline how equity-minded practitioners can use Chicana feminist approaches to create support structures for engineering and computing identity. A support structure can refer to a range of curricular and cocurricular practices, services, programs, initiatives, and policies meant to assist Latina college students as they embody themselves as *caminantes*, progressing through their engineering and computing degree journeys. As a practitioner, you can ease the roads or environments that Latina engineering and computing students endure; you have the ability to clear some of the roadblocks. Support structures can meet a variety of student needs, including academic, social, psychological, emotional, and career needs, and many more.[2] Although support structures may benefit engineering and computing identity at an individual level, their larger influence can collectively uplift Latina students in these fields as a group, too.[3] **The most impactful support structures are those that are not only asset-based and build upon multiple identities and the dynamic nature of identity but also that are situated within the sociohistorical context of Latina students and that ultimately point to a path of knowledge and resistance.**

To start, I focus on support structures related to self- and external recognition in this chapter (outlined in figure 3.1). This chapter provides research-informed recommendations to enhance the recognition experiences of Latinas students

FIGURE 3.1 Generating engineering and computing identity recognition

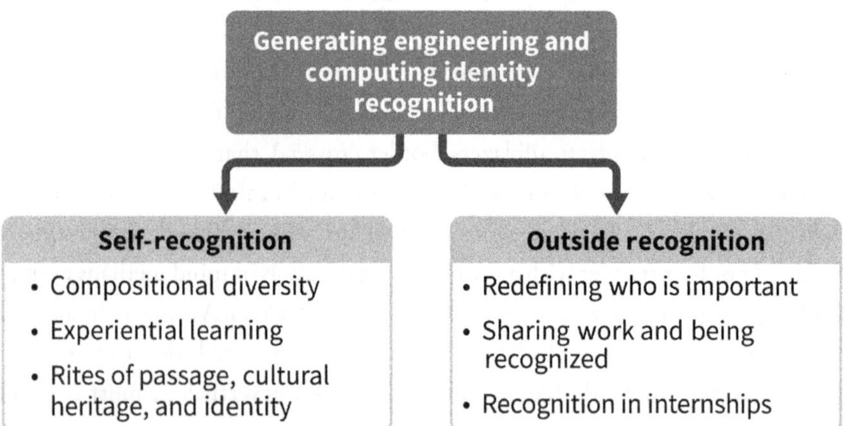

and, in doing so, better shape their engineering and computing identity. In this chapter and the next two chapters, I provide examples of how we might transform current support structures or introduce new ones for greater effect on engineering and computing identity. These examples are not prescriptive but rather a starting place to examine how we create and refine support structures throughout the engineering and computing learning ecosystem to reinforce identity.

When Latina students recognize their own identity as an engineer or computer scientist—and have that identity recognized by others, such as peers and faculty—they are more likely to persist in their discipline and transition to these types of careers. Latina students gain a sense of identity by recognizing themselves as the kind of people who "do" engineering or computing tasks and have a certain kind of mindset.[4] Self-recognition can come in many forms and vary over time and context. Latina students often feel a sense of self-recognition as they acknowledge their own enthusiasm and worldview as engineers and computer scientists.[5] When challenges arise, such as difficulty in classes, self-recognition as an engineer or computer scientist can be compromised.[6]

Outside recognition occurs when other individuals recognize a Latina student as the kind of person who engages in engineering or computing tasks or has this type of mindset. A variety of individuals can serve as sources of outside recognition, including peers, faculty, staff, industry members, and family.[7] These same individuals can also deny recognition and invalidate a Latina student's sense of engineering or computing identity. Moments of self-recognition and outside identity recognition can come in a variety of settings, including both formal and informal contexts (e.g., classrooms, mentor meetings, home, research talks). In many instances, Latina students do not experience self- or outside recognition due to their own negative self-assessments or the devaluing of their engineering and computing identities by others (particularly peers) within these settings.[8] My recommendations for enhancing Latina student engineering and computing identity recognition focus on encouraging both self- and outside recognition.

Within the section on encouraging **self-recognition**, I explore how to:

- **Enhance compositional diversity by:**
  - Hiring more diverse faculty, staff, and leaders
  - Recruiting and retaining more Latina students

- **Promote experiential learning for Latina engineering and computing students by:**
  - Promoting hands-on experiences, community needs, and building on prior knowledge
  - Integrating (and funding) undergraduate research
  - Creating identity-forward professional development opportunities
- **Create rites of passage and encourage cultural heritage and identity by:**
  - Creating and expanding rites of passage
  - Crafting opportunities to encourage cultural heritage and identity
  - Encouraging engagement with identity-based organizations

Within the section on **outside recognition**, I explore how to:

- **Redefine who is important to outside recognition by:**
  - Acknowledging the importance of a range of sources of outside recognition
  - Engaging a range of people who contribute to outside recognition
- **Expand opportunities for Latina students to share work and be recognized both on and off campus by:**
  - Addressing complications of peer identity recognition by men in their classes
  - Integrating poster sessions and community presentations
  - Implementing cross-discipline projects and information sharing
- **Provide opportunities for recognition in engineering and computing internships by:**
  - Scaffolding students and industry partners through the internship process
  - Supporting Latina students as they leverage internship experiences for postgraduation plans

A Chicana feminist approach asks practitioners to create and redefine support structures that facilitate opportunities for Latina students to engage in a range of affirming identity recognition activities that attend to the need for asset-based, contextualized, and dynamic engineering and computing identity. In the next section, I explain more about how these affirming identity experiences can be achieved by encouraging self-recognition and outside recognition opportunities for Latina students in engineering and computing programs.

ENCOURAGING SELF-RECOGNITION FOR ENGINEERING AND COMPUTING STUDENTS

To encourage self-recognition for Latina engineering and computing students, practitioners might consider three sites for enhancement: enhancing compositional diversity, promoting experiential learning opportunities, and creating rites of passage and spaces in which students feel empowered to honor and integrate their cultural heritage and identity. Taking a Chicana feminist approach to self-recognition means leveraging the precious assets that Latina students already embody and emphasizing the journey as a process of becoming that is ever-changing, rather than something that either is or is not achieved. This approach would have us remember that self-recognition is highly contextualized and a reflection of the circumstances and worlds in which Latina students learn and grow, both in our institutions and in our communities. Finally, Chicana feminism would also remind us that self-recognition and the ability to take on a role as an engineer or computer scientist is most promising, both individually and collectively, when it is done on the pathway toward critical consciousness and resistance against white, masculine cultural norms and values. The presence of Latina students is an asset to our institutions and deeply needed as we forge ahead.

When Latina students experience moments of self-recognition, they often feel that they truly have a place within their field, reaffirming their identities and career paths. In many ways, identity is an extremely personal experience in which Latina students have the agency to take up or lay down certain identities—either by choice or due to necessity to survive the environment—as well as the ability to craft their identities as they see fit. These opportunities for self-recognition reinforce the interests they may have sensed since they were young or make them realize, much later, that they are, indeed, holders of engineering and computing identities.

Enhancing Compositional Diversity

To encourage and reinforce identity recognition for Latinas in engineering and computing fields, you, as an equity-minded practitioner, might first consider enhancing compositional diversity within the college engineering and computing environments. This might mean hiring more diverse faculty, staff, and leaders who are not only racially and ethnically diverse themselves but *also* invested in supporting a diverse group of students. You might also explore how you can recruit and retain more diverse students and invest in structures that retain Latina engineering and computing students and encourage them to see themselves in engineering and computing careers.

Leaders might consider **hiring more diverse faculty, staff, and leaders** to support the needs of Latina engineering and computing students and their identity. Doing so, particularly in places where there is opposition to diversity considerations in hiring, may require leaders to take more strategic steps to advertising job positions and networking within organizations, such as the American Association of Hispanics in Higher Education (AAHHE), the Association of Hispanic-Serving Institution Educators (AHSIE), the Society of Hispanic Professional Engineers (SHPE), or other identity-based organizations. In addition, leaders might consider other hiring practices that express to Latin* colleagues that their perspectives are valued, including the requirement of diversity statements, incentives for service to Latin* communities, and resources for culturally sustaining pedagogies. Although compositional diversity among the faculty, staff, and leaders of institutions will not automatically translate into better outcomes for Latina engineering and computing students, seeing individuals who share racial and ethnic backgrounds like theirs is often something that students remark about as a positive aspect of their experience.

Doreen

Growing Computing Identity by Seeing Faculty Members Who Look Like You

Who students see on campus matters. Hiring more diverse faculty can have an impact on how computing students see themselves and their possibilities for engaging in this kind of work. Take the case of Doreen. Doreen had never been interested in technology because she wrote it off as a "guy thing" and "nerdy." She saw computing as something that men mostly did, or if there was a woman doing it, she was nerdy and not cool like she was. She never saw herself as a computing person because it just did not fit with who she was. However, after seeing multiple women faculty members teaching computing courses at her Hispanic-serving community college, she began to change her mind. Never before had she seen women faculty members, particularly those whom she did not inherently see as "nerdy," engage in technology discussions. She loved the way that these female faculty members engaged the class and inspired her interests in the subject. They were regular people doing the kind of work that interested her. For the first time, she saw women role models who brought current, fresh content to class consistently. Also, when concepts were challenging, these women faculty members assuaged Doreen's fears, broke down difficult concepts, and dispelled fears about her performance in the class. Doing so allowed Doreen to develop her interests and take the growth of her knowledge and skills at her own pace. She was finally seeing herself in a computing role. These women faculty members not only helped Doreen to see herself as the kind of person who could engage in computing but also supported her interests and growing competence in the subject area. Now, Doreen feels like she sees artificial intelligence (AI) everywhere and wants to learn more as she moves through her degree.

Beyond mere compositional diversity, you should strive for hiring individuals with a strong social justice orientation—individuals who are committed to serving Latina students in these fields and who seek to see equitable outcomes for them. These are individuals who are committed to creating learning and living environments that support Latina students as well as people who the students might be able to relate to regarding their personal journeys into the field. You can look for individuals who not only take a critical stance on the issues affecting Latina students but also those who are resolute in their desire to take action to solve those issues.

Equity-minded practitioners should also commit to **recruiting more Latina students** to enhance the compositional diversity of engineering and computing spaces. While institutions have vastly increased the number of Latina students who attend college, their numbers remain quite small in engineering and computing majors. Improving the numbers just for numbers' sake is *not* the point. The point is to build a pathway for Latina students and open up opportunities, rather than acting as a gatekeeper of these opportunities.

Therefore, you must consider strategic approaches to recruiting Latina engineering and computing students. This might mean going into Latin* communities and connecting with families and community organizations to build trust and understanding. In addition, you need to offer incentives for Latina engineering and computing students to come into these fields of study, including, for example, the creation of a group of peers who move through the programs together or in clusters. Doing so may help to provide a community to Latina students in engineering and computing fields and encourage them to recognize themselves as the kind of people who engage in engineering and computing work.

While bringing in faculty, staff, leaders, and students is important, **retaining Latina students as well as diverse faculty, staff, and leaders** requires an investment in support structures. For Latina engineering and computing students, these support structures might look like those outlined in other parts of this book, including investing in both overarching structural retention efforts as well as more targeted persistence efforts that support the needs of these students. For Latina engineering and computing students, providing structures for identity performances (e.g., undergraduate research opportunities, structured events, culturally sustaining pedagogies) can lead to opportunities to experience recognition from faculty, staff, leaders, peers, and potential employers. Latina students need structured opportunities to reflect on and craft their identity journeys as they navigate the college process.

To retain diverse faculty, staff, and leaders, institutions may want to consider structures that reward Latin* community investment as well as good teaching and culturally sustaining pedagogies. These are activities that take time and energy, and individuals who engage in these activities should be compensated accordingly. Institutions might incentivize these commitments through augmented tenure and promotion processes, seed funding prospects, extra pay, or release time. Finally, equity-minded practitioners may want to have explicit conversations about opportunities for advancement and how recruitment and retention packages are allocated for diverse hires. Too often, diversity, equity, and inclusion (DEI) work is taken on by diverse faculty, staff, and leaders, which may lead to other institutions recruiting them for better opportunities. Alternatively, if they choose to stay, these individuals may become overwhelmed with their growing DEI responsibilities or simply just tired. In either case, equity-minded practitioners can protect and advocate for individuals doing this kind of work by creating clear structures for reward and retention.

Promoting Experiential Learning for Latina Engineering and Computing Students

Experiential learning is an important piece of crafting an environment that nurtures engineering and computing identity because it not only helps Latina students embody what it means to be an engineer or computer scientist but also encourages them to see themselves in that role long term.

Laboratory, coding, and design projects are crucial experiences that help students become recognized as future engineers or computer scientists. These **hands-on experiences** help students apply their theoretical knowledge to real-world problems, develop practical skills, and build confidence in their abilities. To create and facilitate opportunities for identity recognition, practitioners should invest in large-scale competitions and projects that involve Latina students in engineering and computing work and their communities.

However, these events can be intimidating, invalidating, or outright hostile for Latina students. Reviewing the purpose, goals, and mission of the events may allow leaders to recognize places in which more structured activities could be used to build student competence or enhance recognition opportunities, particularly for Latina students. Latina students who are newer to these concepts may find it difficult to engage and feel recognized in these types of events. However, when practitioners build in structures that enable skills at any level to be meaningfully used and built upon, Latina engineering and computing students are likely to feel more comfortable in these identity recognition spaces.

Equity-minded practitioners might also consider how they can **build on community needs and prior knowledge** to make these events most useful for Latina students. You can build on community needs by leveraging the relationships you have with Latin* communities (more on this in chapter 6) and assessing prior knowledge in a low-stakes way, prior to the events, using a participant survey at the time of registration. Taking these actions signals to Latina students that you are interested in serving their needs in ways that are emergent and community based, rather than prescriptive. Relatedly, you might also consider the location, advertising, and spaces available for hosting these events and how leaders might be strategic in their selections to engage Latina students. You might advertise and hold these events in spaces that are friendly and familiar to Latina students, such as multicultural offices or student centers. Keeping these considerations in mind could enable Latina students to feel a sense of belonging and trust within these spaces, participate in more meaningful identity performances, and be recognized at these events.

Undergraduate research provides valuable opportunities for students to work on real-world problems and develop skills and knowledge that are directly relevant to their future careers. It can also help Latina students gain a sense of identity recognition within the field by providing opportunities to work with faculty and industry professionals and to present their research at conferences. To recruit Latina students, practitioners might use introductory and advanced classes to create and circulate position descriptions so that Latina students could envision themselves getting involved with undergraduate research; describe the project, the lab, the kinds of students you are looking for, and how they can find out more. It is important to share with students that they can reach out to practitioners in a variety of ways, including during office hours or via email, social media, and so on, to discuss these opportunities. Small steps like this help address the sometimes-hidden curriculum that Latina students face as they navigate finding and attaining research opportunities.

Seeking broadening participation or social justice–oriented grants that support undergraduate research efforts and moving toward institutionalization is one way to grow undergraduate research opportunities that are informed by engineering and computing identity concepts. You might first need to increase grant capacity at the institution, including expanding current grant administration staffing or providing more resources to support the available staff members. Equity-minded practitioners, no matter the budgetary situation, cannot fully do the kind of meaningful grant work that is needed without a dedicated team of individuals helping to facilitate the process. If capacity is an issue, consider the creation of excellent resources, including how-to documents, checklists, and guides for best practices in grant-making and make those a part of the orientation process during onboarding. Next, practitioners might consider which funding opportunities provide widespread opportunities or build in research opportunities. This might include National Science Foundation programs, such as the following:

- Louis Stokes Alliances for Minority Participation (LSAMP)
- Hispanic-Serving Institutions (HSI)
- Broadening Participation in Engineering (BPE)

- Broadening Participation in Computing (BPC)
- Racial Equity in STEM Education (EDU Racial Equity)
- Revolutionizing Engineering Departments (RED)

As you consider moving toward institutionalizing research opportunities, you can also explore how research components can be woven throughout the fabric of the curriculum, from mini-research projects within the first-year experience and introductory courses to larger senior design projects and internship requirements. Institutionalization may require a coordinating office on campus dedicated to managing such opportunities across student populations. If that is beyond the capacity of the institution, more integrated efforts within colleges might seek to offer targeted Latina engineering and computing student research opportunities with available faculty or, in the case of community colleges, might connect students to opportunities at four-year institutions.

It is important to understand how Latina students experience self-recognition and outside identity recognition, including how the institution will integrate those concepts into experiences with undergraduate researchers. To support building undergraduate research into the learning experience, equity-minded practitioners might also explore how to create **professional development opportunities centered on identity** for faculty, staff, and leaders. Practitioners might consider ways to familiarize themselves or gain professional development experiences that connect them with basic research around undergraduate scholarship in these areas as well as connect students to identity-affirming experiences. Although training or professional development could be structured in a variety of ways to address localized needs and environments, you might first consider covering basic information about Latina students (chapter 1). Then, connect traditional areas of engineering and computing identity, such as competence and performance, recognition, and interest, with elements of the guiding principles of Chicana feminism (chapter 2). Finally, you could cover actionable activities from parts of this book that you see your institution being able to take to address Latina engineering and computing identity (chapters 3–7) for a multipronged approach (chapter 8) to change.

Creating Rites of Passage and Encouraging Cultural Heritage and Identity

Practitioners should also consider **creating rites of passage** to encourage and reinforce identity recognition for Latina engineering and computing students; this can help these students feel empowered to honor and integrate their cultural heritage and identity. Practitioners might explore instituting rites of passage among Latina students to place greater significance and gravity on a student's progression to and through a degree. Rather than waiting until the end of their educational career for graduation ceremonies, it might be helpful to Latina students to integrate engineering and computing rites of passage throughout the educational experience. In particular, those that involve peers could signal the extent to which a Latina engineering or computing student moves from a new college student to an upper-division student to an engineer or computer scientist. These rites of passage might include specialized ceremonies that hold special significance in connecting students, faculty, and staff or opportunities to engage Latin* families and communities and industry partners in community–institution events.

Practitioners should also look for opportunities to **encourage cultural heritage and identity** throughout the educational journey to enhance engineering and computing identity recognition. For example, practitioners could partner with their local SHPE chapter to elevate college entry and graduation rites of passage that are culturally sustaining and rooted in local communities. A possible college entry rite of passage might look like a welcome and dedication ceremony that invites Latina students (among other students) to recognize themselves as engineers or computer scientists and be introduced to the SHPE community (e.g., students, faculty, local industry employers, families, Latin* community organizations). A possible college graduation rite of passage might look like a similar ceremony to mark the graduation and contributions of Latina student members to the SHPE community, highlight their pathways for the future, and symbolically mark the passing of leadership to the next generation of students. In both instances, local Latin* community organizations could help facilitate rites of passage that are culturally sustaining and further connect Latina engineering and computing students to their communities.

Advisors and other support staff can also support identity recognition for Latina students by encouraging participation in **identity-based organizations** and finding avenues for supporting and promoting these identity-based organizations. Practitioners should consider making every effort to collaborate with these organizations and acknowledge them as valuable spaces for identity growth and recognition. For example, representatives from these organizations might serve on an advisory board providing recommendations. Engineering and computing organizations can provide opportunities for students to connect with other students and professionals, develop leadership and communication skills, and gain hands-on experience through projects and competitions. Latin* or women-centered student organizations also present an opportunity for students to see themselves as engineers or computer scientists, for instance, by talking about their previous research experiences, class projects, or internships. This might look like creating an identity-based organization fair in which engineering and computing organizations, such as SHPE or Tapia, can have significant interaction with Latina students. In addition, advisors and support staff might consider ways to create incentives for or highlight groups taking intersectional approaches to identity-based organization work, such as SHPE's SHPEtinas or the Society of Women Engineers' (SWE)[9] women of color initiative, the Women of Color in Engineering Collaborative.

Lydia

SHPE is Familia: SHPEtinas Nurtures Engineering Identity

Lydia's love for SHPE was palpable as she interviewed. In her final year studying engineering, she was the SHPE president at her predominantly white university. Over the years, her involvement with SHPE has brought her friends and internships and offered her a chance to become a leader of her peers and connect with other Latin* engineers from across the nation. Lydia believed in the power of "SHPE Familia" to create community among Latin* engineering students and be a safe space in which they could face any challenges they might encounter and be in community with other students who look like them and, in many cases, have similar shared experiences. This sense of community was incredibly important to her because most of her family still lived in Mexico, and she needed that support system and tight-knit Latin* community to be successful. SHPE opened her up to new possibilities and support systems and allowed her to meet some of her "best friends" and network with SHPE professionals across the nation, particularly through her SHPE leadership role. And although she loved SHPE, her affection for SHPEtinas, a women's group within SHPE, was even greater. Her involvement with SHPEtinas was a key factor in the shaping of her engineering identity. When she entered college, she knew no

Latina students interested in engineering, even though there were many Latina students at her institution. She has found a support system in these women where they can talk about classes, commiserate about coursework and projects, and inspire each other. She finally saw women who looked like her and who shared many of the same familial and community experiences that she did. SHPEtinas empowered Lydia as a Latina woman to thrive, both in SHPE spaces and beyond.

FACILITATING OUTSIDE RECOGNITION OPPORTUNITIES FOR ENGINEERING AND COMPUTING STUDENTS

Although self-recognition of identity is integral to the process of identifying as an engineer or computer scientist, it is equally important that Latina students gain recognition from others in that role. These experiences occur both on and off campus with a range of meaningful others, including peers, faculty, and staff, as well as families and communities. And although Latina students craft their own identities, all identity exists within existing systems of privilege and oppression and is undergirded by values affirmed (or not) by one's surroundings.[10] Although identity is often considered to be an individual phenomenon in which a Latina student makes sense of her engineering and computing identity experiences, it must also be acknowledged that identity experiences do not occur within a vacuum. Each interaction, activity, and event, as well as the microaggressions and microvalidations, come together in a complicated web of what it means to be recognized by others as engineers or computer scientists. Some "others" may be more or less important to a student's sense of identity. Students may work toward redefining who the significant "others" really are: Are they the traditional institutional players? Or are family and community more important?

To take a Chicana feminist approach to outside recognition means being bold enough to redefine from whom it is important to receive outside recognition by acknowledging the importance of a range of sources and working to engage Latin* families and communities. I also explore in these sections what it looks like to expand opportunities for Latina students to share work and be recognized both on and off campus. For this, you must consider addressing the problem of men in the classroom who may seek to discredit the identities of Latina students and work toward opportunities that allow students to develop their identities, particularly with cross-discipline collaborations and internship opportunities. While these concepts are not new, approaching them through a Chicana feminist lens demonstrates the inherent value of Latina knowledge, skills, and ways of moving through engineering and computing spaces and encourages the world around Latina women to recognize their abilities and identities as future engineers and computer scientists. The result will be Latina students who identify as engineers and computer scientists and who have done so through the help and support of a range of individuals who recognize the assets that they bring to shaping the field, rather than seeking to mold them into the ideal version of who they *think* an engineer or computer scientist should be.

Redefining Who Is Important to Engineering and Computing Recognition

While the importance of Latina students being legitimized by the fields of engineering and computing through their interactions with faculty, staff, and industry partners is indisputable, I want us to pause for a moment to acknowledge that, as we speak, Latina students are **redefining who is important to engineering and computing recognition**. Each year that I do this research, I can say that Latina students are becoming more comfortable with recognizing the indelible influence that their families and communities have on their engineering and computing identities as well as how important it is to them that their communities really *see* them in their role as engineers or computer scientists. Often, family and communities are the first sources of outside recognition. Whether it is recognizing something in Latina children when they are young that is special or turning to them as the go-to for projects or computer fixes when they are older, families and communities recognize their knowledge and skills in ways that are authentic and situated within daily life. For many Latina students, it is also their families and communities who continue to provide support, whether it is academic, social, emotional, or otherwise, long into their college careers because *they* see the promise in their Latina students.

As equity-minded practitioners, you should resist the dominant narrative within STEM education that paints the family or community as somehow less important to Latina students and their identity journeys. In fact, we should be **looking for ways to engage Latin* families and communities** at each step of the identity-building journey and seek them as equal and important partners in this work (more on this in chapter 6). By redefining who is seen as important to the engineering and computing identity process, we are fundamentally shifting power back to Latin* families and communities and recognizing their capacity to shape identities that are multifaceted, dynamic, and products of one's environment.

We can encourage our colleagues to redefine outside recognition in this way by elevating the role of families and communities in our engineering and computing student programming. For example, outreach to Latin* communities should include a component in which campus representatives engage with the families of the Latina students. For K–12 outreach, this looks like inviting Latin* parents with young children onto the college campus or going into the community to share more about engineering and computing educational pathways. Bringing a panel of Latin* family members who already have Latina students studying in these fields could be helpful to connect with the community, answering questions in ways that are relevant and based on the experience of the community. Asking questions about engineering and computing identity could encourage families to share their role in the identity journey both before and after they come on campus.

Sharing Work to Be Recognized Both on and off Campus

An important aspect of facilitating engineering and computing identity recognition is creating **authentic opportunities for Latina students to be recognized by others**, including individuals both on and off campus. When I write about sharing work, what I mean is opportunities for Latina students to take on the role as an expert of their own experiences and demonstrate their knowledge and skills. Often, these opportunities look like giving Latina students the space and capacity to frame problems for themselves, design solutions, and present on the process (individually or within teams). This is *not* merely a throw-away assignment or event, but rather something that Latina students can work toward that is an outward display of all their acquired learning. By providing these authentic opportunities to be recognized by others, you are shifting power back to Latina students and allowing them to be the experts on their own experiences and control the narrative of their projects and learning.

In terms of on-campus moments of recognition, practitioners should consider classroom opportunities and larger community opportunities to recognize Latina students for their work. Within the classroom, practitioners might consider ways in which classroom structures and dynamics might be used to intentionally highlight the work that Latina students do on assignments and projects. Men in their classes have often relegated Latina students to secretarial work or denied them opportunities to engage in the engineering- and computing competency–based work that would have allowed them to feel a greater sense of identity recognition. Identity recognition experiences could be enhanced by **addressing peer identity recognition by men in their classes.** In my research over the years, I have consistently found a lack of identity recognition for Latina students from men.[11] Men have attempted to "spoon-feed" Latina students content, continuously discounted their knowledge and skills, and at times, sought to take credit for their ideas during group projects.

To combat these issues, equity-minded practitioners should consider structured classroom activities that involve rotating leaders within the group or allowing multiple people to engage in the design, coding, or other competency-based work associated with identity recognition. Make sure that, at some point, all students have a chance to lead and that all students take turns being the secretary, administrator, or writer, so that such roles don't get imposed on women in the group and so that all students in your course are able to see themselves using their technical knowledge and being recognized for it. It is very important to think about how you support identity performances. Collaboration and teamwork are essential for success in engineering and computing. Emphasizing and incentivizing teamwork in the classroom can help students develop communication, collaboration, and leadership skills, which are essential for professional practice.

Beyond the classroom, practitioners can facilitate moments of identity recognition. Practitioners might consider partnering up with other courses or other departments to host **poster sessions** in which students go around and view the work of others and comment, creating opportunities for networking and recognition. Inviting people from across the institution could allow students to share their work as well as network with faculty, advisors, and students. To further enrich this activity, you might consider partnering with campus career services offices to reach out to employers who might be interested in hiring engineering and computing students. Rather than a job fair at which students come to employers, a poster session could allow employers to come directly to students. An offshoot of this might be extending the event to include a one-day interview-pairing process in which employers give interviews and offers to Latina students based on their performance at the poster session and students can select from many different offers at the end of the day. This could help shift power back to Latina students and reinforce their ability to see themselves in engineering and computing roles.

Similarly, practitioners might also consider **integrating community presentations** in which students share what they are working on with their communities, preferably the Latin* communities, to address real issues and gain valuable insight. Practitioners might also consider **cross-discipline projects and information sharing**, including partnerships to develop lesson plans, research projects, or interdisciplinary approaches to significant problems. Both approaches push Latina students to extend their networks both within the engineering and computing fields and outside of them. Through these opportunities, Latina students can demonstrate their competence and perform as engineers and computer scientists in ways that feel authentic to them and their communities. These approaches not only provide Latina students opportunities to work with a range of people on engineering and computing tasks but also encourage students to draw upon their courses and previous experiences to be successful. While projects such as these may require significant coordination with cross-discipline and community partners, the influence on outside recognition is important to nurturing a strong engineering and computing identity.

Opportunities for Recognition in Engineering and Computing Internships

Historically, internships have been sites of significant growth for engineering and computing students, particularly as they refine their interests and skills. Internships also offer valuable spaces in which Latina students are recognized as future engineers and computer scientists. To support Latina students on their identity journeys during internships, advisors and support staff can encourage identity performances and subsequent recognition by **scaffolding students and industry partners through the internship process**.

To enhance internship experiences, practitioners can scaffold identity-related resources. Although these resources can address traditional career development content, such as what to expect of an internship, how to get the most out of it, and how to leverage their internship experiences for postgraduation plans, these guides can also include content that specifically addresses intersectional identities and help them work through how they think of their engineering or computing identity before, during, and after the internship. With these resources, students could also explore what sort of work they would like to do in the future that might make them feel more like an engineer or computer scientist. The resources could be worked through with advisors, support staff, or internship employers or in structured internship courses or through online videos.

Connectedly, practitioners can also highlight identity-relevant best practices for industry partners. Although it is important to ask students to think about their identity performances in engineering and computing, it is equally important to educate industry partners about best practices for scaffolding identity performances. Create partnerships for learning with community and industry partners to give students an opportunity to perform their engineering and computing identities. You can tell students all day that they need to get an internship or learn a particular concept or skill, but partnering with industry gives this idea a form of credibility and urgency that students may need. This could involve an ongoing collaborative conversation with employers about how to encourage Latina students to develop their engineering and computing identities through their internship experiences. For example, this might mean reflecting on projects, meetings, presentations, competence, and interactions with others. It might mean training industry partners with these documents as well as providing input from those partners about engineering and computing identity.

In addition, practitioners can consider ways to **support Latina students as they leverage internship experiences for postgraduation plans**. Helping students leverage internship experiences encourages them to consider moments in their internships in which they felt like an engineer or computer scientist and helps them to connect those moments to possible career plans. Advising and support staff should have students complete an activity during or shortly after directed internships that encourages them to make connections between elements of their identities and connects identity development with their postgraduation plans. For example, students might explore who they were before the internship, the activities that they engaged in during the internship, and how those activities shaped the kind of engineer or computer scientist that they hope to become.

CONCLUSION

I will conclude this chapter by going back to how I opened it. Where will you go from here? What bridges will you build to ensure that Latina students can envision themselves as engineers and computer scientists? As Anzaldúa admonishes us, we are the ones that build the bridges as we walk. We are the ones crossing borders and blazing trails. It is up to us to use a Chicana feminist approach to redefine support structures and take a new look at both old and new processes. I will reiterate the important role that you, as an equity-minded practitioner, have on ensuring that Latina students have these opportunities to develop.

You can help Latina students see themselves as engineers and computer scientists through your work with various partners around campus. The overarching takeaway about recognition is that we need to recognize Latina students as holders and creators of knowledge and provide them with opportunities to take on roles as engineers and computer scientists. In the next chapter, I will share more about how you can sustain student engineering and computing interests. After all, without that innate desire to learn more and stay engaged with these fields, recognition in this role can feel stifling or ill-fitting. The role of interest in engineering and computing identity brought Latina students to these fields and can keep them there during the inevitable challenges that may come during their educational journeys.

CHAPTER 4

Supporting Latina Student Engineering and Computing Interests

To the free-thinking Chicana, may I encourage you to assert yourself for the good of everyone "involved" and in particular la raza [the people or the race]. . . . You as a Chicana, are in a unique position of having two and possibly more diverse cultures at your fingertips. You can glean the best of each. You can function easily keeping both feet firmly planted in both worlds, becoming a more versatile and interesting woman.

–Rosalie Flores[1]

The previous chapter outlined how to generate engineering and computing identity recognition and attended to both self-recognition and outside forms of recognition for Latina students. As you have seen, as equity-minded practitioners, it makes a difference what kinds of support structures we put in place to encourage such recognition in meaningful ways. However, to get to recognition, which is incredibly important for Latina students who often face issues of racism, sexism, and other forms of oppression, we must also be concerned with how we support their interests in these fields. As Rosalie Flores inspires us in the quote above, Latina students, for the good of both themselves and *la raza* (the people or the race), should be supported in cultivating their multiple identities and, as this chapter illuminates, in pursing their multiple interests during college that emerge from those multiple identities. As such, as Flores maintains, the cultivation of identities and, subsequently, in this case, career interests can be seen as a benefit not just for Latina students, but for all of our Latin* community.

Growing and sustaining Latina students' interests in ways that are reflective of their authentic, multiple identities are practices that will help them obtain a better engineering and computing identity.

At its core, interest is all about curiosity and a desire to learn more about engineering and computing, a fascination with how things work, and how we can work through complex challenges and build better solutions. In considering these points, we might ask ourselves: How do Latina students become curious about and follow their desires to learn about engineering or computing concepts and careers? They must develop and sustain their interests. The concept of interest encompasses the *types* of interests a student develops (e.g., artificial intelligence, sustainable engineering), the *sources* of those interests (e.g., family, mentors, community), and the *(in)ability to follow those interests over time* due to opportunities and constraints (e.g., within high school and college). Often Latina students develop such interests early in their lives through formal and informal learning opportunities and continue to refine these interests during high school and college and into their computing and engineering careers.[2] However, for other Latina students, these interests may develop much later, such as in the case of community college students, whose interests our team has seen develop as a result of taking introductory computing courses or as shaped by the necessities of their careers (e.g., artificial intelligence and retooling for the future).

Over the past few decades, practitioners have made incredible strides to develop early interests in these areas and support continued refinement of those interests during college. However, many of these approaches reflect a broader identity-evasive approach to change and are not reflective of the unique experiences of Latina students.[3] Further, many of these efforts have been concentrated at the early stages of education rather than supporting the latter stages or various on-ramps or educational pathways that both draw Latina students to engineering and computing initially and sustain their interest over time.[4] My recommendations (outlined in figure 4.1) for building and sustaining interests focus on early and continuing experiences for Latina students. In the section on **encouraging early engineering and computing interests**, I explore how to:

- **Shape course offerings by:**
  - Enhancing introductory engineering and computing courses
  - Offering engineering and computing certificates or minors
  - Promoting college-wide fairs with a focus on these fields

FIGURE 4.1 Supporting Latina student engineering and computing interests

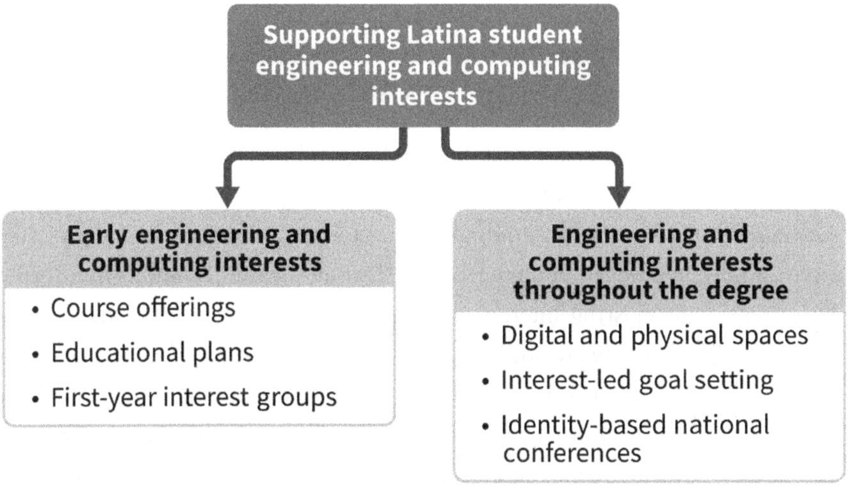

- **Create educational plans that attend to interest development by:**
  - Reinforcing identity
  - Recommending introductory engineering and computing courses as electives
  - Attending to needed flexibility
- **Structure first-year interest groups that center engineering and computing interests and identity by:**
  - Clustering around shared identities and shared experiences
  - Explicitly defining and exploring identity
  - Attending to instructor and guest speaker selection

In the section on **nurturing engineering and computing interests throughout the degree**, I explore how to:

- **Invest in engineering and computing digital and physical spaces by:**
  - Creating digital spaces that are accessible and information rich
  - Investing in physical spaces that connect students with the campus
- **Facilitate interest-led goal setting by:**
  - Assisting students with short- and long-term goals
  - Aligning their interests and goals with the opportunities that exist

- **Fund students' travel to identity-based national conferences by:**
  - Providing funds to Latina students
  - Encouraging engagement with national conferences
  - Fundraising for or in conjunction with Latina students

A Chicana feminist approach to building and sustaining interest asks you to create asset-based support structures that leverage the various identities and sociohistorical contexts surrounding Latina students so that their interests draw from and become woven into the fabric of their lives, families, and communities. Building on the existing interests and situated experiences of Latina students acknowledges that they are not coming into these spaces a blank slate; they bring assets and interests that inherently have value and about which they should be proud. Allowing for fluidity and dynamism within interests over time ensures that Latina students feel as though their identity experiences are expansive in nature and do not foreclose them from exploring and integrating multiple, perhaps seemingly contrasting interests into their engineering and computing experiences. Finally, a Chicana feminist approach to nurturing interests has resistance in its foundation. Whether it is funding students to attend identity-based national conferences or expanding access to course offerings, the foundation of these approaches is the desire to liberate Latina students and empower them to forge new pathways, strengthen the community, and resist marginalization. Nurturing students' interests provides a strong identity-conscious foundation for support structures that encourage Latina students to build on their interests and feel more curious, stimulated, and connected to the engineering and computing work that they do.

EARLY COLLEGE ENGINEERING AND COMPUTING INTERESTS

Enhancing early college engineering and computing identity experiences requires us to consider what kinds of identity experiences students might encounter and how we might enhance those experiences. Early experiences often include high-impact practices related to general student success (such as time-management and study skills), campus information (including navigating campus, important landmarks, and deadlines), and an introduction to career fields (such as engineering or computing). To enhance these introductory experiences, equity-minded practitioners might consider ways to integrate engineering and computing identity into current structures as much as possible or, where needed, to expand or modify those structures. There are opportunities throughout students' early college engineering and computing experiences to infuse culturally relevant and sustaining content as well as highlight the sociohistorical situatedness of the disciplines. In addition, within each of these suggestions, practitioners can intentionally consider how multiple identities and framing as a process of becoming could benefit support structures. The overarching idea is to get Latina students interested in engineering and computing concepts, topics, and resources both at the beginning and throughout their educational journey.

Course Offerings to Expand Early Interest via Access and Exposure

From an identity-building perspective, introductory courses are an important site of growing and maintaining interests. These courses serve an important role in the process of becoming an engineer or computer scientist by introducing the cultural norms, values, and expectations for the fields. They also serve as a key place to nurture early interests and a means for integrating multiple parts of a Latina student's identity and experiences. As such, these courses should be examined to expand early interest.

You might explore ways to enhance **introductory engineering and computing courses** by considering the accessibility of these courses and how they are marketed and experienced by Latina students who may not have previously had engineering and computing exposure. One way to increase the number of Latina students enrolling in these introductory courses is by offering them as general electives available to all students across campus. This would allow Latina students to enroll in them prior to declaring a major. Offering these courses may have a dual benefit: offering these courses speaks to institutional goals of enhancing engineering and computing enrollment and outcomes and also convinces students who might otherwise be on the fence to enroll in them because they will count toward any degree requirements. Comarketing with any existing initiatives around free or subsidized course offerings, particularly in community colleges, could extend the reach of these courses.

Relatedly, making the courses accessible to students without previous engineering and computing exposure allows Latina students who may have interests in the engineering and computing fields, but not prior access, to follow those interests, even if they are undecided about their choice of major. For example, can someone with *no* prior coding experience truly be successful in your introductory computing course? Are the assignments properly scaffolded? What forms of existing knowledge are leveraged in conjunction with learning new skills? How do you assist students who need additional support through the process? These are all important questions to ask as you shape course expectations and implementation.

Georgia

Growing Computing Interests and Identity with Introductory Classes

Georgia, an Afro-Latina from a low-income background, had some interest in tech, but it was not until she took an introductory computing course at a Hispanic-serving community college that those interests and her computing identity truly began to grow. Her local community college offered the class for free, and she followed those initial interests because it was a low-cost, low-risk endeavor. She described her experience as the "smoke and the fog" finally lifting as she progressed through the class. In the beginning, she could see a bit of her interests, but many parts of computing were obscured because she simply had not been exposed to them. As she progressed, she learned more and more about the field, gradually bringing to light not only her computing interests but also her resolve to fully see herself as a computing person. Whereas she had previously been hesitant to fully commit to the computing field by declaring a major, she now felt comfortable pursuing this career. She credited much of her computing identity support to her instructor who made her feel comfortable with asking questions and who made computing assignments fun and interesting for her, despite her being new to the field. As a result of this class, she decided to pursue a computing career and challenge herself to see what she could do, both technically and creatively, in her educational journey.

Regarding course offerings, another possibility might be to **offer engineering and computing certificates or minors** to encourage Latina students to cultivate their engineering and computing interests and lay the foundation for possible transitions to these majors. Although they may differ according to institutional context and requirements, certificates or minors could be a set of agreed-upon courses (perhaps around eight to eighteen credit hours) that provide Latina students with an idea of what the field looks like. Certificates or minors could allow undecided Latina students to explore engineering and computing topics in a structured and defined way as well as offer something tangible to future employers who value these skill sets. Similarly, certificates or minors create an opportunity for Latina students in other, perhaps related majors to augment their own experiences to gain a more specialized form of knowledge. Rather than having to leave their original major (e.g., business, nursing, environmental science), Latina students can gain skills and knowledge that will prepare them for the workforce or graduate education.

Miami Dade College

Artificial Intelligence Awareness and Artificial Intelligence Practitioner Certificates, Miami, Florida

Full disclosure: I am a co-principal investigator on a current Hispanic-serving institution (HSI) grant with Miami Dade College (MDC) for the creation of these certificates. However, even if I were not, I still believe that the path MDC has taken in the creation of these certificates is an example of how community colleges and higher education institutions more generally can meet the growing artificial intelligence (AI) workforce needs, get students interested in computing careers, and facilitate computing identity development. In creating their college credit certificates (CCCs), MDC, one of the nation's largest HSIs, sought to expand computing pathways and train their faculty and staff for the ever-changing world that is AI. MDC is a unique institution that awards certificates, associates degrees, and bachelor's degrees to ensure that students, particularly those from Miami-Dade County, have access to high-quality and affordable postsecondary education.

To meet the current workforce needs of the greater Miami area, which many contend is pushing to become the next US AI and computing hub, MDC has created two certificate programs aimed at getting students plugged into AI and expanding their AI knowledge. The nine-credit **Artificial Intelligence Awareness Certificate** requires no previous background in technology and offers fundamental AI competencies, including an introduction to AI thinking, ethics, and an applied elective (e.g., AI in business).

The eighteen-credit **Artificial Intelligence Practitioner Certificate** focuses on applying machine learning tools, natural language processing, computer vision, and ethics and social responsibility. This certificate is a stackable credential that connects with the associate and bachelor's AI degrees at MDC and typically takes one year or less to complete. Each of the certificates is enhanced by MDC's AI Center, which supports students, faculty, staff, and the community across multiple campuses to engage more fully with AI through a series of professional training, partnerships, and events. What I love about MDC's approach is how they have attended to the needs of two different kinds of learners—the novice and the more experienced—to meet students where they are with their interests. In our study of students in these courses, we found that the courses encouraged Latina students to grow their interests in multiple ways and build a stronger computing identity.[5]

In addition to course offerings, certificates, and minors, equity-minded practitioners might consider also promoting **college-wide fairs with a focus on engineering and computing** to draw in Latina students who are undecided or considering switching their majors. Unique to this opportunity, students would have the chance to connect with departments in smaller, more intimate settings focused on building interests and skills within a given field. These kinds of opportunities may encourage Latina students not only to follow their interests but also to build relationships with departments for long-term identity development and success. To prepare for such events, it is important to emphasize the nature of these fairs as identity-building spaces and encourage departmental colleagues to see this opportunity as a means not only for increasing student enrollment but also, more importantly, for individual student development of their identity. For the actual fair itself, you might consider requiring departments to showcase the following elements (on a board or handouts or other representations) to help Latina students envision themselves in the department and within those future careers:

- What kind of engineer or computer scientists they hope the student will become
- What a day in the life of a typical student in this department looks like

- What future careers students can expect from this program
- What communities the programs serve or what problems they are trying to tackle

All of this will encourage students to match their own interests to those of the department and the field, as well as push departments to be explicit about their norms, values, and outcomes.

Creating Educational Plans That Attend to Interest Development

Over time, the creation and institution of educational plans have become almost commonplace in higher education. As a high-impact practice, many students will create educational plans early in their engineering and computing college journeys. These educational plans typically include what courses a student must take, course sequencing, prerequisite requirements, transfer intent (for community college students), and co-op or service requirements, among others.

Equity-minded practitioners are essential partners who can assist Latina students in creating **educational plans that reinforce their engineering and computing identity**. I advocate for attending to interest development within these educational plans and revisiting them each year with students to account for changes in interests and attending to the multiple, intersecting identities of students. Attending to interest development within these educational plans might look like asking students to identify areas that spark their curiosity or causes that are important to them that could be worked into course planning, internships, co-ops, service requirements, or the like.

At their core, educational plans can give equity-minded practitioners an opportunity to **recommend introductory engineering and computing courses**. Practitioners might recommend an introductory course in AI or cybersecurity, for example, to students from a variety of educational backgrounds and not separate these fields from other fields. Students may become interested in computing and engineering as a result of exposure to concepts they might never have encountered, so an opportunity to try these courses early might mean increased interest or the discovery of a way to integrate engineering and computing into areas they had not originally thought of, such as integrating AI into business or art. Recruiting students to these courses might involve distributing flyers or screen prompts around the campus to promote introduction to engineering or computing courses, making special efforts to consider what draws people in, and exploring what the industries in the area currently need.

Creating **flexibility and tailoring educational plans** to student interests is vital. Revisiting the educational plan each year allows students the chance to revise or refine their interests as a reflection of the experiences that they had in the previous year. Although students can already take these actions, making this a formal part of the culture of advising and supporting students signals to them that consideration of one's own interests, rather than just those of employers or the institution, is valuable in the creation of an engineering or computing identity that is authentic to them. While I do not advocate for completely ignoring one's workforce landscape, I do advocate for a more balanced approach to ensure that Latina students are not forced to become versions of themselves that they do not even recognize because of continuous suppression of their own interests. This often results in students who, despite completing a degree, may become disenchanted with the field or their job because it is not aligned with their interests.

New Mexico State University

Engineering Education Enrichment (e3) Initiative, Las Cruces, New Mexico

If you are looking for an example of how to encourage engineering interests, you might consider the **Engineering Education Enrichment (e3) Initiative**, led by **Dr. Patricia Sullivan, Associate Dean for Outreach and Recruitment in the College of Engineering**, especially if you are looking for ways to tailor learning and meet growing industry needs. The e3 Initiative is a project-based, hands-on learning experience for undergraduate students at New Mexico State University, a large Hispanic-serving institution. The e3 Initiative connects students with industry-valued certifications, entrepreneurship training, and design project experiences to make them career ready. The initiative works with industry partners to align student skills and opportunities with employer needs while balancing students' ability to become self-directed adult learners by allowing them to choose from a variety of activities. Any student who is a US citizen or permanent resident with a 2.0 grade point average (GPA) or above is eligible for the program. Once engaged with e3, students choose from three learning tracks: certifications (i.e., to build and demonstrate skills), entrepreneurship training (i.e., to gain skills around product development), or individual/group design projects (i.e., to execute a client-based project). Certifications might include those related to AI, machine learning, SolidWorks, or business foundations; entrepreneur training could include topics such as Studio G, cultivating an entrepreneurial mindset, e-commerce, or starting your own business; and individual/group projects have ranged from those involving Bluetooth technology, wind turbines, and accessible playgrounds to those that deal with microbreweries and low-carbon-footprint food trucks. Mentors associated with e3 engage with training to familiarize themselves with mentoring best practices, learning philosophies, and mentorship as leadership. Assessments show that the e3 Initiative has had a positive influence on student engineering identity, including enhancing students' ability to be recognized as engineers by faculty, peers, and family.

Dr. Antonio "Tony" Garcia, former Principal Investigator of the e3 Initiative at New Mexico State University, now retired from academia and engaged as a freelance bionanotechnology inventor and consultant, credits much of the success of this initiative to removing barriers to programmatic participation (e.g., GPA requirements, using matching funds for expansion) and evaluating engineering programming in identity-forward ways. Over time, he has found that allowing for a flexible and kind of "pick-your-own-journey" approach to engineering development has appealed to Latina students and allowed them, among others, to create their own pathways to become the kinds of engineers that they want to become and form their own unique engineering identities. What I love about this initiative is that it allows Latina students, among others, the agency to shape their role as engineers by tailoring it to an experience that aligns with their career goals and interests.

Structuring First-Year Interest Groups That Center Engineering and Computing Interests and Identity

You might consider ways to structure **first-year interest groups (FIGs)** that center engineering and computing interests and identity. FIGs could be structured in a variety of ways, but I suggest a combination of cohort-based classes in which students take two to four classes together during their first semester and attend a seminar led by a peer mentor and faculty or staff facilitator. These elements could also be coupled with various activities to further connect mentors and first-year students. **FIGs could be clustered around identity, majors, shared experiences, or special topics in engineering and computing** to allow Latina students to self-select into those that are most salient to their interests and identity. FIGs may provide a space in which Latina students see others who look like them or who have had shared experiences prior to college. Likewise, these groups may serve to bring out the assets of Latina students, build community, and promote a sense of belonging. FIGs aimed at engineering and computing interests may encourage Latina students' identity, particularly if those FIGs connect them with other Latina, Latin*, or women students who share similar identities or experiences. FIGs also encourage exploration of diverse engineering and computing disciplines to discover their specific interests and strengths. Practitioners should also consider connecting with identity-only interest groups to promote engineering and computing majors and opportunities to spark interest.

To address engineering and computing identity within FIGs, consider **explicitly defining and exploring identity**, rather than leaving it to chance. Whether the FIG is identity based or topically based, you have the option to integrate an identity approach to the subject in a variety of ways. For example, if it is a Latina-based engineering FIG, you can integrate topics focused on what it means to be a Latina engineer, including what interests students might have and how they see those interests influencing their current educational pathway or future careers. If the course is based on a topic, such as one concerned with civil engineering and water-based challenges and solutions, you might consider how the course might attend to the sociohistorical culture of the region, including the identities of the individuals who have resided on the land, both historically and currently. This could also spark conversations about how students became interested in civil engineering and how they see these interests in their future. In any case, explicitly tying content to a learning objective related to identity can encourage both instructors and students to continue to center identity throughout the course.

Relatedly, who leads and visits FIGs matters. **Attending to instructor and guest speaker selection** can shape interests associated with engineering and computing identity. Special consideration should be given to those who facilitate FIGs because such groups can be defining contexts in which Latina students decide to continue with (or enter) engineering and computing. We must place in these positions dynamic and caring faculty, staff, and student members who attend to gender, race, and other identity-based concerns as well as those who center culturally sustaining practices. Individuals who are familiar with culturally sustaining practices can look for opportunities to transform the learning experience into something that honors and leverages the various identities of Latina students and pushes them to develop their engineering and computing identity.

Inviting Latina guest speakers who work in the engineering and computing fields is another important option to consider as you structure FIGs. Latina guest speakers can help students understand the different career paths that are available to them, share how current employees navigated their educational and career journeys, provide insights into the day-to-day work of engineers and computer scientists, and offer advice on how to succeed in these fields, particularly in light of the often hostile climates that Latinas may encounter. These guest speakers could serve as potential role models or mentors to students. Another added benefit is that by inviting Latina guest speakers, institutions communicate to students and to the field that Latina ways of knowing are valued. In addition, the act of inviting Latina guest speakers to campus, particularly at high-visibility events, communicates to the larger campus community that the campus cares about diversity, equity, and inclusion (DEI) and representation.

NURTURING ENGINEERING AND COMPUTING INTERESTS THROUGHOUT THE DEGREE

While encouraging Latina students to build their engineering and computing interests early in their experiences is essential, it is also important to support those interests throughout the degree-earning process. To do so, practitioners might consider investing in engineering and computing digital and physical spaces and nurturing interest-led goal setting by funding student travel to conferences to connect student interests to the broader engineering and computing fields.

Investing in Engineering and Computing Digital and Physical Spaces to Inspire Interests

Practitioners should consider investing in **engineering and computing digital and physical spaces** to support interests throughout their Latina students' educational careers.

Digital spaces for Latina students are paramount to how they receive information and understand the values of their institution throughout their engineering and computing journeys. Digital spaces are often the first impression that engineering and computing programs have on Latina students. They convey who the institution serves in their programs as well as communicate the norms, values, and direction of the field. By creating digital spaces in which Latina students can find information and programming that is unique to them (as well as linking to important resources that are not Latina specific), these students will know that their institutions are receptive to their needs and seek to support them on their engineering and computing identity journeys. Latina students may notice whether there are people who look like them reflected in digital spaces as well as what identities or experiences are elevated as important to the educational experience. In particular, digital spaces may be especially important to Latina students who are learning online or hybrid, have a disability, are commuter students, or have a range of other intersecting identities that may limit their physical time on campus. How we structure digital spaces and the content that we put on these pages are important to how we convey the importance and belonging of Latina students to engineering and computing spaces and should be evaluated and refined to encourage students to envision themselves both in the program and in the larger field.

While both digital and physical spaces are incredibly important to the identities of students, **physical spaces** represent a significant financial and symbolic commitment that conveys that engineering and computing fields matter. Financially, these spaces mean that institutions are directing funding and resources toward these efforts. Symbolically, these spaces can be areas in which Latina students connect with engineering and computing concepts, resources, and other people. At their core, physical spaces are also a way for you, as equity-minded practitioners, to ensure that Latina students are reflected in the sociohistorical context of the institution and become part of the fabric of who the institution is at an organizational level.

Well-curated physical spaces offer Latina students information about engineering and computing fields, open up conversations for garnering more information, and connect them with similarly interested faculty and peers. Creating these spaces with Latina students in mind reminds us to think about the images and messages that are crafted throughout the space. As plans are drawn up for physical spaces, as equity-minded practitioners, you might consider working with the Latin* faculty or staff associations or Latin* student groups, particularly those in engineering and computing if possible, to ensure that their needs and concerns are integrated. There may be opportunities to integrate images or messages that directly speak to Latina students or Latin* communities and encourage interests in these fields.

Facilitating Interest-Led Goal Setting

To continue nurturing identity throughout the educational journey, equity-minded practitioners can also build and sustain interests through meaningful goal-setting conversations with Latina students. When practitioners facilitate activities on short-term goals, students are able to build upon existing interests as well as realize longer-term goals. Practitioners can help students to set and achieve **short-term goals** by utilizing advising and support structures throughout the institution. They can also encourage students to think about SMART (specific, measurable, achievable, realistic, and time-bound) identity-based goals and who their supporters are along the way, drawing on both their institutional and home communities. Inspired by George Doran's work on crafting SMART goals,[6] I suggest taking SMART goals and creating an experience in which students explore identity in similar goal-setting ways. For example, consider activities that encourage students to think about short-term identity-based goals in this way:

- **Specific:** Goals are narrowly tailored to what a Latina student seeks to accomplish in terms of their identity during college. For example, does a student want to be a Latin* community–informed engineer? Then their experiences might include gaining community service hours, participating in urban planning activities or courses, or taking an internship related to these interests.
- **Measurable:** Goals are designed around measures that will show progress toward the goal. Continuing the example, Latina students might demonstrate success through gaining a certificate in urban planning or attaining a set number of community service hours each year to demonstrate their commitment to the community and stay connected. It might also be helpful to guide students to measure success using engineering and computing identity measures, such as acquisition of knowledge and skills, recognition from various sources, and refinement of interests over time through a range of experiences.

- **Attainable:** Goals are reasonable to complete within a given time frame. Although Latina students might be tempted to take on many goals, you could guide them toward more attainable goals by encouraging them to consider responsibilities, timelines, and interests. While I do not advocate for getting students to *change* their goals, I do think that a discussion about attainability and timelines is a healthy one to prevent unnecessary anxiety and stress.
- **Relevant:** Goals are connected to a student's values and overall trajectory. It might be helpful for Latina students to create a graphic organizer in which they align their goals, values, and overall trajectory to ensure that they see the connections between the pieces of their experiences and become good at telling that story as a part of their identity journey and career preparation. Keeping students focused on relevance of their goals can also encourage them to seek out experiences that are in line with their trajectory or find creative ways to integrate opportunities that they are afforded into how they tell their story.
- **Time-based:** Time-based goals are goals that have an end date so that a student may prioritize tasks. Although identity is a continuously evolving part of the student experience, it benefits students to think about certain time points (e.g., end of first semester, end of first year) and where they would like to be in crafting their engineering and computing identities at those points. Likewise, building in opportunities for reflection at those times will ensure that Latina students continue to meet their goals and modify their trajectory as needed.

While general goal setting is often woven into first-year experience courses, SMART identity-based goals are more defined and can lead to enhanced engineering and computing identity. They might encourage students to consider how their interests influence their goals and vice versa and demonstrate a clearer path to linking interests to careers. Rather than relegating SMART identity-based goals only to first-year experiences, these types of exercises can be helpful when intentionally incorporated throughout the educational experience.

In addition to short-term goal setting, equity-minded practitioners can also encourage students to focus on their **long-term goals**, particularly during challenges along the educational journey. You can help students to cope if their long-term goals must shift or could benefit from considering what makes sense for their journeys and desires. Too often, Latina students feel that their engineering and computing interests and goals are growing further away from their day-to-day experiences. Encouraging students to map out their long-term career goals and strategize toward those goals will enable Latina students to see how their actions and decisions today can keep them connected to their aspirations for the future. Practitioners should also consider creating opportunities for long-term goal setting so that students can reflect on how their goals are connected to the needs and desires of their families and communities and who they want to be in the future.

For example, professionally, a Latina student wants to eventually assume a leadership position at a cloud-based computing company, like Amazon Web Services (AWS) or Cisco Cloud Solutions, but also seeks to stay connected to her home community, whether she lives there or contributes in some other way. Long-term goal setting involves working with the student to identify all of the intermediary steps that would be involved in reaching these goals, including evaluating what kinds of pre- and postgraduation steps would put her on this path, such as considerations of how each step will grow her interests, where she wants to live, what kind of lifestyle she wishes to have, and how often and in what ways she wants to connect to her home community, including through (what remains of) employee resource groups with potential employers or other means. At its foundation, being identity conscious in long-term planning means being inclusive of the whole person, not just the engineering and computing identity part of the students. Blending both personal and professional interests into long-term goals encourages Latina students to bring their whole selves to the process and recognize the connections that both sides have to one's engineering and computing identity.

Equity-minded practitioners might also help students to continue to refine their interests in engineering and computing by **aligning their interests and goals with the opportunities that exist** in each educational setting. Goal-setting activities can act as a sort of web, encouraging students to consider the many interests that they have and how they can activate their current networks to inform their goals. You might encourage students to ideate without boundaries and then cocreate ways to find alignment among their interests, goals, and opportunities. The goal here would be to get students to dig deep into their experience to understand what truly interests them about engineering and computing careers, including what excites them about this kind of work and how they see themselves in this role. Consideration should be given to opportunities that exist both within and outside of the institution as well as what to do if students' interests do not align with their current setting. Such goal-setting activities can be integrated into existing academic support services, student success programming, or current DEI efforts. It could be as elaborate as creating digital systems or integrating an app that connects student interests and goals with career opportunities, or as simple as encouraging students to do this as part of a comprehensive approach to student support services.

Funding Student Travel to Identity-Based Conferences to Stimulate and Sustain Career Interests

Beyond the institution, I encourage equity-minded practitioners to consider how they will fund student travel to identity-based engineering and computing conferences. Conferences are a significant opportunity for learning, with unique opportunities to explore one's niche interests that may not be covered in the general curriculum. Identity-based conferences also provide a safe space for students to nurture interests and build community with people who look like them. Whether it is Latina students specifically, the Latin* engineering or computing community more broadly, or STEM or women's conferences even more broadly, these spaces not only offer a place to meet and be immersed in the energy of those who look or think similarly but also are an opportunity for Latina students to build a stronger sense of identity and resistance against white, masculine norms that undergird these fields. Gathering together in these spaces signals to institutions, companies, and the world that Latina students are capable of assuming engineering and computing roles and encourages Latina students to redefine what engagement in these organizations looks like and how they can exist in these spaces.

Possible conferences might include, but are not limited to, the following:

- Society for Hispanic Professional Engineers (SHPE)
- Society for Advancement of Chicanos/Hispanics and Native Americans in Science (SACNAS)
- AnitaB.org's Grace Hopper Celebration (GHC)
- Tapia Conference for Broadening Participation in Computing Through the Center for Minorities and People with Disabilities in Information Technology/Association for Computing Machinery (CMD-IT/ACM)
- National Center for Women and Information Technology (NCWIT)

At some of these conferences, there are also opportunities specific to Latina students, such as connecting with SHPEtinas within SHPE and Technolochicas within NCWIT. Each of these conferences provides a space in which Latina students can understand and be proud of their engineering and computing identities as well as connect with other Latina students, faculty, staff, and employers in these fields. These conferences are committed to equity within these fields but, more importantly, acknowledge the importance of identity in shaping one's educational and career journeys.

Equity-minded practitioners must explore **making the institutional financial commitment to fund student travel to professional conferences**, particularly those that are identity based and encourage students to develop their interests in a culturally sustaining way. Providing funding to students for conference travel communicates that institutions value their presence at the institution and wish to support their interests. It also signals to Latina students that the institution is willing to make a financial contribution to enhance their experience in culturally affirming ways. Moreover, it communicates with employers that the institution is committed to identity-affirming DEI efforts. Conferences provide an opportunity to network with peers, potential future graduate school faculty, and those who can offer future internship or employment opportunities.

Funding students to go to these events involves making a concerted effort to demonstrate the benefit of **engagement with the national level of identity-based conferences** to students' engineering and computing identity journey and future job prospects. While some students need little convincing that this kind of opportunity is worthwhile, others may need more persuading, particularly those who see networking as artificial, inauthentic, or drastically in contrast to their nature (shout-out to my fellow Latina introverts!). If this is the case, it is on us to demonstrate how identity-based national conferences provide a space to craft one's identity and create real connections with other students who share similar experiences. These spaces can also be seen as an extension to students' current community and a place to meet with employers who truly care about individuals from their backgrounds. You might highlight that there are various ways to nurture one's interests in involvement with identity-based national conferences, whether it is the technical side that one desires or the community-based elements. Likewise, practitioners might highlight leadership opportunities in these organizations that often culminate with the annual national conference or a chance to shape the field and create long-term connections that could help with job prospects.

Cecilia

Institutional Support of Computing Identity via Conferences and Hack-a-Thons

Many of the Latina students I have interviewed over the years have commented on the power of traveling to large-scale events as a boost to their engineering and computing identities. These events, whether or not they are Latina specific, provide valuable spaces for identity development. Cecilia, a recent graduate and now software engineer, fondly recalled how the Grace Hopper Celebration (GHC), one of the nation's largest gatherings of women in computing, and an all–Mexican women AnitaB Hack-a-Thon opened up her computing identity possibilities. Even though she was interested in computing at the beginning of college, the only reason she officially declared her major was because she wanted to go on the all-expenses-paid GHC trip. What resulted from that event was a transformative experience in which she saw so many other women in computing and learned more about her own computing identity and pathway. While she was not initially sure what path she wanted to take after college (i.e., graduate school or industry), the GHC helped her learn about those options and connect with others who had made similar choices. Ultimately, the GHC also provided her with internship experiences that put her on the industry path and helped her gradually take up her role as a software engineer. Later in college, she even took up a "mother hen" role in helping other women attend GHC, get the most out of it, and build a community of women in computing. Similarly, her institutionally sponsored trip to an all-Mexican women AnitaB Hack-a-Thon was an incredible experience in which she was able to build community and see so many other women who looked like her. Looking around at all of the Latina faces and experiencing the deep level of computing knowledge and skills energized and inspired her. Given her educational context of a predominantly white institution, her involvement with this event encouraged her to see herself in a computing role and create connections with other Latinas.

Finally, sometimes budgets are severely limited, and sending students to conferences may not seem possible. However, I encourage you to consider **fundraising for or in conjunction with Latina students** to allocate scholarships that cover the costs of conference attendance. Collaborate with your endowment office, express your need, and see if they can identify donors (alumni or corporate). You can also write letters to prospective donors directly or consider an annual fundraising event to raise money for the conference scholarship fund. In addition to their national conferences, many organizations may also hold smaller regional conferences and workshops, which can be more financially feasible if budgets are tight. These experiences can still be tailored to Latina students by inviting the campus SHPE chapter to send Latina delegates or, while at the conference, having structured briefings and debriefings to help students get the most out of their conference experience, including how the event could help shape their identity as an engineer or computer scientist. You might also consider how to support students as they fundraise for the conference for their organization's members. For instance, while the institution might not be able to send all SHPE students to the national conference, they could provide seed money or space or facilitate industry partner connections so that students can advocate for funding for their own organization. While institutional funding signals commitment, in the absence of this, Latina students can still be a galvanizing force for ensuring that SHPE members make it to the national conference and see their identities grow as a result.

CONCLUSION

This chapter focused on structures for supporting Latina student engineering and computing interests, both at the beginning of and throughout the college experience. I explored how early interests could be cultivated by shaping course offerings, creating educational plans that attended to interest development, and structuring first-year interest groups that center engineering and computing interests. I also examined how to nurture engineering and computing interests throughout a student's educational career by investing in digital and physical spaces, facilitating interest-led goal setting, and funding student travel to identity-based national conferences. The next chapter will continue to build on the importance of support structures by outlining major ways that you, as an equity-minded practitioner, can build elements of competence and performance into engineering and computing experiences.

CHAPTER 5

Building Latina Student Competence and Performance in Engineering and Computing

Sometimes it seems there is so much in the world that needs to change, I am overwhelmed before I get started if I think of what I cannot do. I am encouraged and filled with hope when I realize what I am capable of doing as one human being and how much I have done.

–Sandra Cisneros[1]

The previous chapter focused on supporting the engineering and computing interests of Latina students. Students must be interested enough in the fields to get them through the enrollment door and persist in their studies until graduation. However, as you probably well know, interest is not enough to sustain Latina students through the often-challenging worlds of engineering and computing. During college, Latina students must become competent in their field and be able to perform in the role of an engineer or a computer scientist to be successful. It may seem like a colossal task to think about all the knowledge, skills, and experiences that Latina students need in order take up these roles and the many changes needed to make all those elements more identity forward and affirming to these students. But, as Sandra Cisneros reminds us in her quote above, we need not despair about everything that needs to change and become disheartened by what we cannot do. We must focus on what we can do and, indeed, what we, as equity-minded practitioners, have done to encourage engineering and computing identity for these students. By doing this, we can find the joy and hope needed to improve Latina student competence and performance in these fields.

Competence and performance refer to how engineering and computing students acquire and grow their technical knowledge and skills as well as their ability to apply those skills in real-life situations. Latina students enter and move through college gaining a variety of forms of disciplinary knowledge and skills depending on their prior exposure to the content at school, at work, or in their communities. Many practitioners associate Latina students' competence and performance with deficit-based thinking and attempt to "fix" students by emphasizing their lack of knowledge or devaluing their ways of knowing and identity.[2] Too often, Latina students are asked to build upon their knowledge and skills without acknowledgement that the richest learning comes when it is contextualized within the sociohistorical context and attends to the multiple identities Latina students embody.[3] A Chicana feminist–informed approach asks practitioners to consider how they can build on the existing assets of students, including their multiple and dynamic identities, to encourage engineering and computing identity experiences that support Latina students' success.[4] This includes building on the ways of knowing and forms of capital that Latina students bring with them and enhancing identity opportunities within classrooms and support services.[5]

My recommendations (outlined in figure 5.1) for building student competence and performance in engineering and computing focus on improving classrooms and support services.

In the section on classrooms, I explore how to:

- **Uplift knowledge cocreation by:**
  - Paying attention to who has power within the classroom setting
  - Maintaining an open channel of communication
  - Providing ample opportunities for feedback to peers and instructors
- **Introduce and scaffold key concepts and remain flexible by:**
  - Normalizing the building of foundational skills at the college level
  - Building in open space to the course agenda
  - Creating smaller connected and supported tasks throughout the course

FIGURE 5.1 Building Latina student competence and performance in engineering and computing

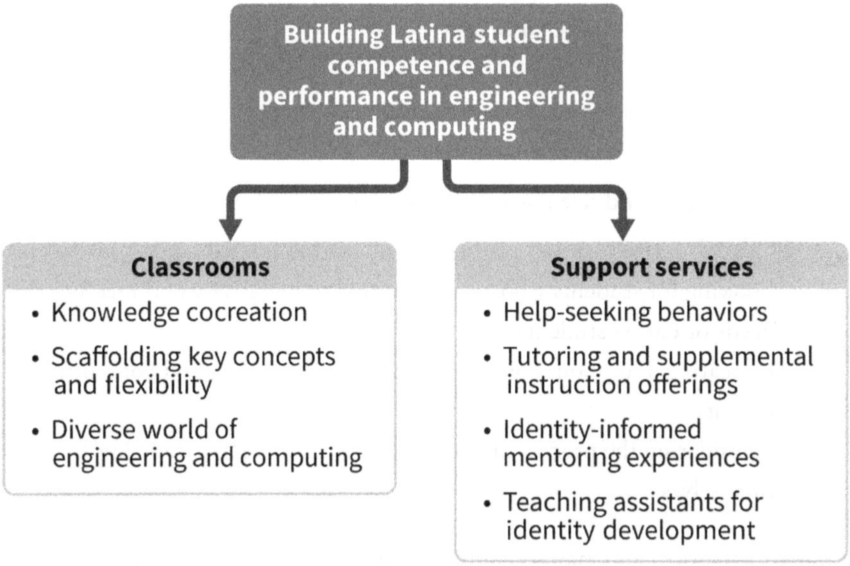

- **Integrate the diverse world of engineering and computing surrounding students by:**
    - Using diverse examples
    - Highlighting diverse career opportunities
    - Incorporating real-world applications and partnerships

In the section on support services, I explore how to:

- **Address help-seeking behaviors by:**
    - Fostering a culture where seeking help is normalized and supported
    - Integrating support services into the college experience
    - Connecting students with academic and social resources
- **Build out tutoring and supplemental instruction (SI) offerings by:**
    - Redefining these activities as identity-building spaces
    - Evaluating current offerings for opportunities to serve Latina students
    - Encouraging more Latina students to serve as tutors and SI leaders

- **Commit to meaningful identity-informed mentoring experiences by:**
  - Creating or modifying existing mentoring programs
  - Setting explicit expectations, activities, and assessments that forefront identity
  - Crafting mentoring experiences around opportunities to assume the role of engineer or computer scientist
- **Select, train, and use teaching assistants (TAs) for identity development by:**
  - Looking for students who are committed to inclusivity and meeting the needs of Latina students
  - Educating TAs about concepts related to engineering and computing identity
  - Considering the process of becoming that TAs are experiencing themselves

ENHANCING COMPETENCE AND PERFORMANCE IN ENGINEERING AND COMPUTING CLASSROOMS

Instructors have a unique ability to either affirm or inhibit the development of engineering and computing identities in the classroom as a function of the way that they approach their classrooms and the topics that they teach. It is important to think of the classroom as a primary place where Latina students absorb the norms, values, and required competencies for the fields they pursue as well as shape how they will engage with their field both now and in the future. The following recommendations are aimed not just at faculty members but anyone who engages with students within a classroom setting.

A Chicana feminist approach to classroom settings would have us not only attend to the multiple and dynamic identity-building processes that occur in these spaces but also find ways to examine how our own courses may be supporting or inhibiting Latina students from gaining competence and performing their identities. An emphasis on what Latina students bring with them to the classroom from their prior experiences and the communities around them can connect and reinforce the technical content that they are learning and form a site for future resistance against oppressions.

Uplifting Knowledge Cocreation in Engineering and Computing Classrooms

Equity-minded practitioners should consider how they involve students in the knowledge cocreation process. Cocreation of knowledge means that both students and the instructor are involved in shaping the classroom experience. Providing space within the classroom and curriculum development to engage with **knowledge cocreation** can enable engineering and computing students to be involved in the learning process rather than serve as passive consumers of knowledge. Allowing Latina students to suggest areas that are of importance to them, express forms of knowledge that might traditionally be discounted, and determine what knowledge and solutions are needed can increase their engagement and be beneficial to their identity.

For example, an introductory computing class could approach its artificial intelligence (AI) unit by having Latina students suggest key AI topics that they find interesting or important to their future careers. Then, the faculty member could encourage students to think about how their school, family, and community experiences have informed what they know about the need for AI or its possible applications in the field. These reflections could be used as a basis for tailoring curriculum and assignments as well as facilitating group interactions and project-based learning. While knowledge cocreation might not be solely Latina focused in any class, this approach allows Latin* ways of knowing to be honored among the many voices of students within the class.

Paying attention to who has power within the classroom setting may enable practitioners to balance that power so that students truly are investing in their own knowledge creation. Attending to power encourages Latina students to engage with, feel invested in, and be connected to their learning spaces. They can start to see themselves reflected in their coursework and begin to break down the distance between students and their learning environments.

Part of knowledge cocreation is allowing for an **open channel of communication** between the students and their instructor. When practitioners seek to collaborate with Latina students on such knowledge cocreation, they should consider giving students opportunities to wield power in the classroom. This can be done through activities such as creating shared values and guidelines for classroom or project engagement. In this way, the instructor serves as more of a facilitator on the journey with their class than a lecturer in the dated "sage on the stage" model. As a result of this framing, practitioners acknowledge and honor the greater Latin* communities' ways of knowing, including ways that might not be traditionally considered valuable to engineering and computing contexts.

The structure of the peer and professor feedback matters, too. You should **provide ample opportunities for feedback to peers and instructors** alike. Feedback ensures that Latina students have an opportunity to voice their concerns and have their needs met, which is incredibly important to facilitating the acquisition of knowledge and skills. As the adage goes, closed mouths do not get fed, and in this case, if we do not provide a space in which mouths can be open and expressive, we are essentially not feeding our students what they need to be successful. The process of gaining feedback can be as high tech or low tech as needed, so long as students feel as though they are being heard and that their feedback is being integrated in a meaningful way. For example, students could provide peer feedback on the structure and process of group projects, and they could provide the professor with feedback via a formative assessment midsemester, allowing suggestions to be integrated into the latter part of the class.

Introducing and Scaffolding Key Concepts and Remaining Flexible

Teaching and curriculum design might be improved by **attending to how we introduce new content and build foundational skills** within engineering and computing. For many students, how they encounter new content and build foundational skills in these areas can mean the difference between whether or not they stay in their fields. As such, equity-minded practitioners should teach students how to embrace these processes and make learning these foundational concepts more accessible.

Doing this requires meeting students where they are and **normalizing the building of foundational skills at the collegiate level**. Practitioners should acknowledge that Latina students—like all students—may come in at different levels of competence and performance throughout their experience. We cannot make assumptions about students' level of experience with certain concepts or how they *should* have developed their skills prior to getting into college or coming to our classes. Research shows that Latina students often become interested in engineering and computing at the end of high school or when they enter college, unlike many of their peers. Before that, they were often pursuing a different interest or moving in a different direction based on what was going on in their community or the industry needs around them.

Given this, instructors must be flexible in their classrooms. Instructors can do this by **building open space into the course agenda**. With all of the topics that must be covered and the pressure to know more and more, you must resist the urge to completely fill every space in the course agenda with material. Resist the urge to pack every moment of your time together with readings, problem sets, coding assignments, and group activities so that there ends up being no time for expansive thinking or flexibility. Instead, build in the time for meeting Latina students' needs. Flexibility tells Latina students that educators are committed to meeting students where they are and to promoting continuous learning and the building of strong foundation skills.

To support the building of strong foundational skills, you might consider how to integrate guided, scaffolded learning experiences into courses by **creating smaller connected and supported tasks throughout the course**. Latina students could work up to larger projects with intermediate tasks due at different points of the term so that students can receive feedback on the project along the way. Scaffolded learning experiences can enhance students' technical competence and provide the ability for them to become recognized in their fields by giving them an opportunity to build on prior knowledge. Scaffolding a student's learning gradually allows them to become more independent. Scaffolding is another way of telling students, "You can do it, and I'm here to help." Over the course of the semester, scaffolds are taken away so that students are able to do more on their own.

Demi

Developing Computing Identity by Meeting Students Where They Are

Rather than assume that Latina students come to us with fully formed computing identities, it is our responsibility to meet students where they are at in order to support that identity development. Demi, a multiracial, first-generation Latina college student at a Hispanic-serving community college, had originally attended college at a university, but as she described it, "life happened" and she left the university. The community college offered her the ability to work full time and go back to college. Although Demi never saw herself as a computer scientist, an institutional scholarship encouraged her to take an introductory computing course focused on AI. While the course was billed as introductory, it soon became evident that it was not, in fact, introductory. Demi needed basic Python skills that she did not have and worried that she would be unable to complete the course. Demi was drowning in a sea of homework assignments, and many of her project teammates were dropping the class. Without help, she feared that she would also have to drop the class. However, her professor took notice, took the time to restructure the class because many individuals were struggling, and gave the students the tools that they needed to be successful. This meant being flexible enough to go back over foundational concepts, provide additional resources, and provide in-class time to go through coding and design exercises. She felt that her professor went above and beyond to ensure that she and others understood how to manage the course and work with the knowledge that she had as she acquired more programming skills. Although her computing identity was minimal before the course, she saw it grow as she became more interested in AI and computing concepts and found that she could apply that knowledge to problem-solving and computing projects. While Demi still struggles to see herself in a computing role, she has been able to remain in the introductory computing course and has even signed up for another computing course. Given her identity journey even within one course, the future looks promising for her to one day take on a computing role.

Integrating the Diverse World of Engineering and Computing Surrounding Students

Using diverse examples and real-world connections is a tangible way for equity-minded practitioners to make real-world connections to the classroom and curriculum for Latina students. **Use of diverse examples**, particularly related to issues that concern Latin* communities, signals to students that the instructor is not only invested in their ability to connect and apply learning to broader engineering and computing contexts but is also committed to affirming the identities of their students and acknowledging a broad range of applications of traditional engineering and computing concepts. You might consider how the course content may relate to Latin* communities, particularly those that are nearby, or find examples of Latinas or other Latin* causes, issues, or concerns related to the content. Instructors can do this by highlighting diverse career paths within engineering, incorporating real-world applications and partnerships, and using examples that are aligned to Latin* communities.

Engineering and computing are broad fields with many different career paths. **Highlighting the diverse career opportunities** within engineering and computing can help students understand the many different ways they can apply their skills and identity within their field. Many Latina students in our studies have felt as though their educational experiences prepared them for careers that they, fundamentally, did not seek to engage with and that the concepts they learned and the career opportunities that they were exposed to did not reflect the values that they held or the communities that they wished to serve.[6] Highlighting a broad range of engineering and computing career opportunities allows Latina students to make connections between what they are learning and the ability to apply those skills to careers that they feel better reflect the kind of engineer or computer scientist that they wish to become, rather than who someone tells them to be. When featuring career opportunities within class, you might focus on how you can build upon the multiple, intersecting identities of your Latina students as well as validate that there are many different types of careers in engineering or computing. Whether you have small or large classes, you could take a short survey or a classroom poll on the first day of class in which you ask about the kinds of careers that students might like to hear about, as well as particular issues, parts of the country, or world challenges that students are interested in.

Practitioners might also consider ways to **incorporate real-world applications and partnerships** into the engineering and computing learning experience. Real-world applications can help students understand the relevance of their coursework and see how they can apply their engineering skills to solve real-world problems. Building partnerships with Latin*-centered organizations or corporations focused on recruiting Latina students could be an opportunity for institutions to show they are committed not only to highlighting diverse career opportunities but also to investing in partnerships that will result in Latina students entering careers that reflect who they are. See chapter 4 for more information about how to build and sustain relationships that can maximize your ability to bring real-world applications into your classroom.

Pennsylvania State University Berks

Engineering Ahead, Reading, Pennsylvania

At Penn State, Engineering Ahead (EA) is a group of National Science Foundation summer programs serving underrepresented STEM (science, technology, engineering, and mathematics) students on multiple campuses. Now in its ninth year, EA at Penn State Berks is a free, first-year student, summer academic enhancement program that aims to create a support system for incoming underrepresented engineering students from diverse socioeconomic and cultural backgrounds to ensure success in college. Each year, approximately twenty students engage in a four-week residential summer experience focused on math readiness and a first-year, two-semester STEM persistence experience. These classroom experiences are focused on scaffolding the learning experience and providing a solid foundation for understanding that students will build on as they transition into the university. EA builds professional development and college success skills through a series of programming, including corporate engineering company tours, engineering design–oriented community service, scholarship support, and engagement with current Penn State engineering students and alumni. As such, EA exposes students to real-world engineering challenges and hands-on work and highlights a wide range of possible career opportunities.

The program has resulted in significantly higher grades and fewer dropouts in students' first college math course as well as higher first-year grade point averages (GPAs) and university retention. Likewise, students, most of whom hold minoritized identities such as being a first-generation college student, a low-income student, and/or a woman, emerge from the experience looking like a "different" kind of first-year engineering student because of these experiences, making them competitive for internships and possessing a greater sense of their engineering identity. As **Dr. Ryan Hassler, a teaching professor of mathematics and coordinator of EA at Penn State Berks**, explains, undergirding all this work is the idea that engineering students, including Latinas, exist at the center of multiple, intersecting, and dynamic identities that influence their engineering experiences. Through attending to identity-nurturing experiences, EA enables students to refine their interests, build skills, and see themselves as engineers. What I love about this program is that it attends to multiple elements of engineering identity, including a commitment to growing interests and skills, and seeks to place students in opportunities to perform and be recognized by faculty, peers, industry partners, and the community for their engineering identities.

In concluding this section, I want to reiterate the important role that instructors play in building competence and performance opportunities for Latina students. Classrooms are a key space in which Latina students connect with the worlds of engineering and computing and discover how they will exist within these fields. As we turn to the next section on support services, it is my hope that these two sides of the house—academic and support services—can become more integrated for a seamless identity experience for Latina students.

COMPETENCE AND PERFORMANCE IN SUPPORT SERVICES FOR ENGINEERING AND COMPUTING LATINA STUDENTS

When practitioners attend to issues of competence and performance in support services for engineering and computing Latina students, it can enhance how students experience their lives beyond the bounds of the academic classroom. In addition to instructors, advisors and other support staff play an integral role in supporting engineering and computing identity by structuring meaningful opportunities for Latina students to demonstrate and refine their competence and performance as they progress through their degree. It is often in these spaces that Latina students can be vulnerable and gain a larger perspective on their experiences. In addition, it is also within these spaces that practitioners unpack the process of becoming an engineer or computer scientist and support Latina students so they can overcome the challenges associated with persisting in these fields.

A Chicana feminist approach to support services is one in which we see services that allow for Latina students to live authentically both inside and outside of the classroom while gaining the knowledge and skills that they need. Improving support services for competence and performance is all about integrating support into the lived common college experiences of Latina students and redefining how our institutional services can speak to the Latina identity-building process.

Addressing Help-Seeking Behaviors of Latina Students

To address help seeking for Latina students, equity-minded practitioners must **foster a culture where seeking help is normalized and supported.** It is normal for students to seek help. Practitioners should encourage this: when instructors foster a culture where seeking help is normalized, Latina students build both technical and navigational competence. This point is about meeting students where they are, without judgement, and connecting them with the academic and social resources that they need to succeed. Students will come to view advising and support services as integral parts of the college experience and will use them as part of being a reflective student when they are woven into the fabric of the educational experience.

Advising and support staff might consider how they can **integrate support services** into the college experience. For example, when a student signs up for classes, resources such as existing supplemental instruction (SI) or tutoring could be automatically recommended to students. This would enable students to immediately understand the SI and tutoring resources available to them along with the class. Better yet, institutions might look to how they can create embedded tutoring systems within courses, particularly challenging and/or introductory courses. This might enhance efforts of faculty members by allowing them to gain a greater sense of student mastery of the material as well as refine curricular decisions and available resources.

In addition, practitioners might consider how they **connect Latina students with academic and social resources.** Consider creating an interactive map for students of how to access resources and who to go to for help in building their competence. This could include having a ready list of resources that is shared with all advisors or support staff. It might be as simple as a web-based list that is periodically updated or as elaborate as a quiz in which students can indicate what kinds of academic and social resources they are looking for and a web-based platform that helps guide them to those resources, including clear information about locations, contacts, and websites.

Building Out Tutoring and Supplemental Instruction Offerings

To enhance competence and performance, you might consider building out tutoring and SI offerings. Building out these offerings does not simply mean adding or growing offerings but considering the offerings in terms of what they can do to support engineering and computing identity development. This might mean **redefining these activities as identity-building spaces**, rather than just a means of improving outcomes. Are those not the same? Not entirely. Tutoring and SI have the possibility to become important sites of identity competence and performance as Latina students build and reinforce their own competence (taking advantage of the opportunities themselves), as well as sites in which they assume their identities as engineers and computer scientists (by serving as tutors and supplemental instructors). Redefining the space can force you to examine what values are inherent in these activities, including both content and overall approach.

Relatedly, equity-minded practitioners might seek to **evaluate current offerings for opportunities to serve Latina students**. Rather than simply increasing the level of services offered, a more data-informed approach could be taken to analyze what courses in particular might benefit from improvement for Latina students. This might mean looking at data in a variety ways (e.g., by race, gender, first-generation college student status, disability) in order to get a clear picture of how to serve Latina students and their multiple intersections of identities. Once you have a good idea of where to grow these initiatives, you might consider ways to **encourage more Latina students to serve as tutors and SI leaders**.

Building out tutoring and SI offerings, particularly for courses that are often challenging for Latina students, can provide students a place where they can build their knowledge and skills and address academic issues as they arise. Teaching someone to do something requires you to have a clear understanding of a concept and to be able to break it down for another person. One benefit of building out tutoring and SI is that it creates an opportunity to have more Latina students serve as tutoring and SI instructors as a means of developing their own ability to perform and demonstrate their competence as engineers and computer scientists. Consider the effect it would have if you recommend a student to be a tutor or SI instructor, saying, "Hey, you're really good at this. Why don't you become a tutor for this subject? You could really do that." Sometimes that turns on a light bulb: "Oh, I'm good. I'm good at this. I can be an engineer because I'm good at this." This gives students an opportunity to help other students and to really see themselves as the kind of people who do engineering and computing work. Enhancing tutoring and SI can also bring to light areas where support services might need to shift to adjust to changing needs of Latina students as well as the broader student population.

Committing to Meaningful, Identity-Informed Mentoring Experiences

Equity-minded practitioners might look to mentoring experiences as identity-building spaces for Latina students. Mentoring can be a valuable way for you to help students develop a sense of belonging and identity within the field of engineering. Providing mentorship opportunities can help students connect with experienced engineers who can provide guidance, support, and advice on how to succeed in the field. Providing role models and mentors who have succeeded in engineering can help build students' identity within the field and provide guidance and support as they navigate their academic and professional journeys. Mentoring spaces are not traditionally thought of as identity-building spaces, particularly for boosting competence and performance, but more as spaces for community building.

However, we can reconceptualize these spaces as places that encourage students to grow their skills and perform their engineering and computing identities. This might mean looking across mentoring spaces to think about ways to shift them toward engineering and computing identity. Practitioners might **create or modify existing mentoring programs to enable Latina students to fully realize and step into their identities** as Latina engineers and computer scientists. Practitioners can create mentoring spaces that allow students to take on the role of engineers and computer scientists as well as dually encourage their mentees' identities.

Creating a mentoring program that helps foster identity might involve **setting explicit expectations, activities, and assessments that forefront identity**. You can align mentoring programs with the four major areas associated with engineering and computing identity (interest, competence, performance, and recognition). For example, you could think about how you could make mentoring programs, whether peer to peer or mentor to mentee, more focused on individuals assuming engineering and computing roles. You could take the opportunity at the beginning of a mentoring initiative to set explicit expectations around how the mentoring experience is a process of becoming and structure activities and assessments that attend to each of the identity measures.

To attend to identity, practitioners could **craft mentoring experiences around opportunities to assume the role of engineer or computer scientist**, whether it is through structured research or service projects. In this way, Latina students could build their identities by gaining valuable knowledge and skills while being mentored through the process of assuming their role in the field. Mentor-to-mentee mentoring programs could do this by focusing activities that get engineering and computing Latina students engaged in projects that place them in the role of an engineer or computer scientist who works on a real-life, community-based project and receives feedback from their mentor. Important to this process is creating documents or trainings for mentors that encourage them to understand identity-informed methods to mentoring and make a commitment to guiding their Latina student mentee in their identity journey.

Selecting, Training, and Using Teaching Assistants for Identity Development

Similar to tutoring, SI, and mentoring programs, the role of teaching assistants (TAs) can be integral to supporting how students build competence and perform their engineering and computing identities. Practitioners delve deeper into the selection, training, and utilization of TAs as affirmers of engineering and computing identity and teaching assistantships as positions that can be used to reinforce the identity of the Latina students who occupy them. In terms of selecting TAs, practitioners should **look for students who are committed to inclusivity and meeting the needs of Latina students** and who are competent in the content area. This sets a tone for how the class will function and how students in the class build their competence. Inviting Latina students to become TAs can provide them a space to perform their identities.

In addition, practitioners might also consider **educating TAs about concepts related to engineering and computing identity**. Familiarize TAs with the components of a professional identity in this area and explore ways that both the faculty member and the TAs can support these identities. Soliciting feedback from the TAs can help practitioners keep a clear pulse on student needs and how to better meet students where they are.

Finally, practitioners could consider using TA responsibilities not only to encourage identity in other students but also to encourage the **process of becoming that the TAs themselves experience**. TAs are performing their engineering and computing identities as they help other students. Practitioners should consider implementing plans in which TAs receive feedback on their own demonstration of competence and performance and go through scaffolding processes to support their own identity.

In concluding this section, I would like to point out the key role that support service individuals have in ensuring that Latina students are supported in their process of becoming. You all are doing fantastic work that bridges so many experiences for students and makes gaining and sustaining an engineering or computing identity possible. While much identity development takes place in the classroom, I believe that just as much takes place outside of it, and we have a duty to Latina students to ensure that their experience is as fully integrated as possible.

CONCLUSION

This chapter focused on building Latina student competence and performance in engineering and computing. We explored how improving competence and performance in the classroom might involve uplifting knowledge cocreation, introducing and scaffolding key concepts and remaining flexible, and integrating the diverse world of engineering and computing surrounding students. We also examined how equity-minded practitioners might look toward improving help-seeking behaviors and tutoring and SI offerings, as well as modifying mentoring experiences and teaching assistantship processes. Although the past three chapters have focused on the importance of support structures for Latina students in these fields, the next chapter will focus on the relationships needed to make these structures possible. None of us can do this alone, and it is only by looking to those around us that we can seek to make lasting change.

CHAPTER 6

Creating and Sustaining the Relationships Needed for Developing Engineering and Computing Identity

But one voice is not enough, nor two, although this is where dialogue begins. . . . The real power, as you and I well know, is collective. I can't afford to be afraid of you, nor you of me. If it takes head-on collisions, let's do it: this polite timidity is killing us.

–Cherríe L. Moraga[1]

To build the needed support structures for engineering and computing identity for Latina students, you must first nurture the relationships needed to do the work. Some equity-minded practitioners—often well-meaning and with hearts and minds dedicated to change—may jump headfirst into what support structures are needed and how we engage in immediate action. However, it is the relationships among students, faculty, administrators, industry partners, and communities that will enable those structures to endure, particularly during challenging times. These relationships demonstrate your investment in Latina students and their engineering or computing journeys as well as their hopes, fears, and challenges.

Cherríe Moraga's words remind us that it takes more than just one person to engage in a dialogue and create a collective. Moraga's writings have always spoken to me on both a personal and professional level. A queer, mixed-race Chicana feminist, Moraga feels like one of my mentors urging me to consider the complexities of the identities that people hold as well as the need to harness the collective power of our communities, even when that path requires us to give much of ourselves. We cannot be afraid of each other. We cannot hide in polite timidity. To build and sustain the relationships needed for developing engineering and computing identity, equity-minded practitioners must simultaneously be willing to make themselves vulnerable and have the courage and confidence to go beyond reluctance or fear of consequences to truly connect both with Latina engineering and computing students and the communities they are a part of.

This chapter was both the easiest and hardest to write. I love relationship building (even though I am *deeply* introverted), and I like to think of myself as a natural people connector, often guided by a relationship-focused orientation to all aspects of my life. For this book, I want you to understand that good support structures (and resistance efforts, but more on that later) are often the work of tireless equity-minded practitioners acting as a collective, not individually. And, while there may be champions for Latina engineering and computing students, as there often are, equity-minded practitioners cannot remain the sole champions for the cause. Collective action is necessary to sustain your efforts for students beyond your immediate sphere of influence or time within an institution.

The difficult aspect of writing this chapter was discerning how to impart the idea that relationship building is something that can be learned and refined over time through a series of foundational understandings and good practices and, simultaneously, possesses a kind of magical element that defies words. It is almost more of an art form: it needs to be done authentically and spiritually, and to be truly transformative, it needs to be done in tandem with deep reflection and approached with a spirit of humility and a desire to learn. It is from this standpoint that I share with you how you, as an equity-minded practitioner, should build and sustain the relationships needed for developing engineering and computing identity.

Outlined in figure 6.1, I believe that we can amplify these interests through nurturing relationships that support Latina students as complex individuals as well as expand competence and performance through relationship building that is dynamic and responsive to Latina students and their communities. A Chicana feminist approach encourages practitioners to become intersectional thinkers, moving between and among groups and partnerships to inform the engineering and computing identity work needed to be done. You can address the dynamic

FIGURE 6.1 Creating and sustaining the relationships needed for developing engineering and computing identity

Amplifying interests through relationships that support Latina students as complex individuals	Expanding competence and performance through relationship building that is dynamic and responsive to Latina students and their communities	Intensifying recognition opportunities through creating relationships that respect history, culture, and Latina ways of knowing
☐	☐	☐
☐ Becoming an intersectional identity thinker	☐ Addressing the real problems	☐ Immersing yourself in the Chicano Movement and an ethos of Chicana feminism
☐ Acknowledging that multiple identities result in multiple interests	☐ Listening first, acting second	☐ Blurring the lines between the institution and Latin* communities
☐ Thinking beyond the usual partners	☐ Responding to shifting issues	☐ Question: Who are we asking Latina students to become?

nature of identity work by acknowledging the underlying issues of deficit-based thinking and by listening to Latina students, honoring their ways of knowing, and remaining receptive and flexible in their learning. Furthermore, I believe that practitioners can intensify recognition opportunities through creating relationships that respect history, culture, and Latina ways of knowing. By gaining better knowledge of the Chicano Movement and Chicana feminism as well as connecting to families and communities, practitioners can better understand the worlds in which Latina students exist.

AMPLIFYING INTERESTS THROUGH RELATIONSHIPS THAT SUPPORT LATINA STUDENTS AS COMPLEX INDIVIDUALS

Relationship building has the capacity not only to amplify interests in engineering and computing fields but also to provide opportunities to recognize Latina students as complex individuals. However, how best to inspire those interests while balancing the needs of faculty, administrators, and industry partners as well as those of the nation and the world often eludes even the most thoughtful problem-solver. Engineers and computer scientists like to solve complex, intricate problems, and what is more complex than individuals and groups with all of their individual and collective needs?

Relationship building for Latina students in engineering and computing must attend to the complicated and interrelated nature of identity. Latina students are not a monolith; they represent a variety of experiences and have complex needs and desires for the future.[2] In Gloria Anzaldúa's essay "La Prieta," she pushes back against the notion that she is merely defined by her Chicana identity—rather than being seen for her complex identity as a dark-skinned queer feminist woman—remarking that the world around her "would chop [her] up into little fragments and tag each piece with a label."[3] Likewise, we cannot merely attend to one identity or look to one set of relationships to enhance engineering and computing identity. We must move in multiple directions to meet the multifaceted nature of identity for our students.

Chicana feminism would not have us essentialize the experiences of our Latina students—and neither would the students. Year after year, I hear from a range of Latina engineering and computing students—spanning geography, discipline, and institution—that they resist a monolithic approach to their engineering and computing identity.[4] Latina students derive their interests from a variety of sources, including teachers, mentors, peers, families, and communities, and they embody a range of complex identities.[5] As such, we must become intersectional identity thinkers and relationship builders, recognizing that multiple identities result in multiple interests (and multiple oppressions) that must push us to think beyond our usual partners to support identity. My recommendations for amplifying interests focus on supporting Latina students as complex individuals. Within this section, I explore how to:

- **Become an intersectional identity thinker by:**
    - Moving in many circles
    - Putting in the work to connect, not divide
- **Acknowledge that multiple identities result in multiple interests by:**
    - Representing identities and interests within the curriculum
    - Creating interdisciplinary relationships
- **Think beyond the usual partners by:**
    - Knowing your Latina engineering and computing students
    - Seeking interest convergence

Become an Intersectional Identity Thinker

Becoming an **intersectional identity thinker** requires us to first reckon with the fact that Latina students in engineering and computing resist definition in so many ways. As a group, Latina students are diverse, coming from a range of backgrounds, countries, languages, values, and customs. They come from over twenty-one different countries, such as Mexico, El Salvador, Honduras, and Guatemala, and speak a range of languages, including English, Spanish, and

Portuguese, but also many others such as Quechua, the Incas' language heard near the Andes, or Guarani in Paraguay. Some Latina students have just arrived from their home countries or were brought as children to the United States, whereas others have been in this country for generations.

Furthermore, Latina engineering and computing students not only possess a variety of differing identities but also are affected by a range of intersectional oppressions, depending on the identities they hold and the salience of those identities within the contexts in which they live and attend college. For example, a first-generation, low-income Latina college student might encounter different challenges than a continuing-generation, high-income Latina college student, even if both are in engineering or computing. Becoming an intersectional identity thinker requires us to build relationships by moving in many circles, putting in the work to connect rather than divide, and connecting with other intersectional identity thinkers.

Move in Many Circles. Chicana feminism is clear on the **importance of relationships and coalition building**. It is far too easy to stay comfortable doing one kind of work, in one kind of way, with one set of people. Yet, if you are to step into work that is transformative, you must move outside of your traditional circles. You must be willing to make yourself (potentially) uncomfortable to grow and expand your understanding. Becoming an intersectional identity thinker requires that we begin to move in many circles so that we are exposed to a variety of ideas and ways of knowing as well as become versed in the needs and desires of many communities.

What do I mean by "move" in many circles? This might look like **considering the various intersectional identities that Latina students have** and looking for ways to understand and support those identities. You could listen to webinars, attend lectures, collaborate on projects, or cross-promote or cosponsor events—anything that gets you connecting with individuals and groups that you might not normally connect with Latina students and their engineering or computing identities. For example, rather than moving in only Latin* or other circles serving racially and ethnically marginalized students, equity-minded practitioners should step out of their comfort zones to move in circles that care about other issues related to immigration, LGBTQ+ experiences, or socioeconomic status. Likewise, on campus, practitioners might look to work with disability services to foster support for a range of abilities, or off campus, community colleges could be good partners in expanding pathways to engineering and computing.

Courtney

Computing Identity in All of Its Complex Beauty

To serve Latina students, we must be willing to first see and understand their multiple, intersectional identities and then think creatively about how to build relationships in order to meet those needs. Courtney has been one of my most interesting research participants yet. Her unpacking of her computing identity demonstrated to me the complexity of a single individual. An admitted introvert and shy woman, Courtney was nervous to take part in the study and, before we started, related that she was unsure if her story was the kind of story I was looking for because she was not the typical computing student. Little did I know what was ahead. During her interview, when asked to bring in artifacts that described her computing identity, she brought in pictures of a half-wolf, half-Indian woman; a semi-naked woman with an owl; Ada Lovelace (arguably the first woman computer scientist); and the Virgin Mary. Now, you might be wondering what all of these seemingly disparate artifacts could possibly mean for her computing identity. As she explained, the half-wolf, half-Indian woman photo was related to her mother's indigenous roots and the powerful nature of women as shapeshifters (a common theme in Chicana feminism). The semi-naked woman with an owl reminded her that her computing identity was wrapped up in feminine energy and mysticism that made her unafraid of the challenges and her male peers. The Ada Lovelace picture connected to her gender identity and feelings of being a pioneer for little girls of color who want to be in computing. The Virgin Mary was meant to symbolize the idea that her gender, spiritual, and computing identities mutually reinforced each other. I was blown away by how she had made sense of and demonstrated the connections between her various identities, especially at such a relatively young age. She articulated a kind of synergy between her various identities that made her success within computing at a large, research-intensive, predominantly white university possible. Courtney's multiple identities fused together to make her computing identity complex and highly inspired by a feminine energy and rootedness within the spiritual realm. This gave her power and agency to overcome a variety of personal and educational challenges that were placed before her to continue building her computing identity and persist within the field. As such, if we are to think creatively in her case about possible partners, we might consider groups that have gender, spiritual, and computing expertise on campus. This might mean looking toward colleagues in women and gender studies or computing education as well as interfaith offices or Chican* studies to see how we might better serve our Latina students.

Moving in many circles allows not only for **personal and collective intellectual understanding** to become enriched but also for practitioners to connect with people with whom they might not interact on a regular basis and who might, in the future, become resources either for ourselves or for our Latina students. Not only does this attend to the nature of intersectional identities, but it also shows Latina students that they are seen and cared about as people.

Put in the Work to Connect, Not Divide. Latina students in engineering and computing do not live single-issue lives, and their interests are not the result of one way of living and interacting with the world. It is our **responsibility to listen to and learn from each other**. As resources become more and more scarce—even for the engineering and computing fields, which have, historically, been able to weather higher education's shrinking budgets—it becomes even more imperative that we seek out connections rather than divisions. Rather than dividing and scrounging for crumbs, it behooves us to continue **connecting and steeling ourselves to weather the ideological or financial threats** that may arise in our efforts to serve and nurture the interests of Latina students in these fields.

The metaphor of the bridge in the book *This Bridge Called My Back* is meant to simultaneously symbolize the way-making that women of color do to make connections between seeming contradictions and complexities and indicate the pain that is experienced in carrying this burden. It is our responsibility to "lay down the planks to crossover onto a new place"—like *This Bridge Called My Back* did—to get us to somewhere new and better where we can continue collectively moving toward a more expansive view of interests and greater equity for Latina engineering and computing students.[6] Rather than laying down planks alone, equity-minded practitioners should consider connecting with other intersectional identity thinkers.

To connect with other intersectional identity thinkers, **consider multiple facets of your own identity** that you will leverage in your work to support the identity development of Latina students. Are you an ardent supporter of first-generation college students because you, yourself, were a first-generation college student? Consider how you might bring greater awareness of how first-generation college student issues might *also* differently impact Latina students because of historic and contemporary racism. Are you committed to rural education and student success? Then you might look for ways to connect rural initiatives to Latina students in engineering and computing, such as rural programming that integrates Latina ways of knowing or connects rural K–12 Latina students with their higher education counterparts. In any case, relationship building between intersectional thinkers can help find creative solutions to the complex identity problems that our students face on a day-to-day basis in their efforts to nurture their interests.

Multiple Identities Result in Multiple Interests

At first pass, the idea that multiple identities result in multiple interests is an easy one to understand. People have a range of identities that make them who they are. Most would agree that these identities manifest in a range of activities (e.g., hobbies, readings) that inspire curiosity and take up space in both peoples' minds and calendars. For example, Latina students coming from international backgrounds may be interested in international issues or immigration policy, so they volunteer with organizations that champion these causes. Other Latina students may be in disciplines that are overwhelmingly male dominated and, as a result, are acutely aware of their gender identity, so they get involved with women's organizations, particularly related to their discipline or field.

Identities and Interests Within the Curriculum. The more complicated part is the acknowledgement that Latina students, because of their multiple identities, should have an innate ability to **pursue their multiple interests in tandem with their engineering and computing program experiences.** In fields that often boast some of the most "rigorous" (I use quotes because I believe in the rigor of any field) and complex degree programs, with little room to follow interests or tailor one's experience, the idea of interest-led experiences is at best looked at with skepticism and at worst with contempt.

I see the ability to integrate multiple interests as having two important purposes for engineering and computing identity for Latina students. First, when a Latina student has the agency to integrate *her* interests in *her* degree plan in a way that works for *her*, she is more likely to feel a sense of identity and investment in the work that she is doing. Many Latina students struggle to see the connections between coursework and the interests that they have, but providing some flexibility within the curriculum will give Latina students the opportunity to shape their own engineering and computing identities while remaining competitive in future careers.

Second, the **ability to integrate multiple interests into a normally rigid degree plan is an act of resistance**—a disruption to engineering and computing disciplines—that upholds and honors Latina student ways of knowing. To integrate multiple interests, practitioners should consider how relationship building can not only bridge the gaps between institutional silos and encourage students to leverage their multiple interests in creative ways but also establish more sustained interdisciplinary relationships. First, institutions must recognize the added value that comes with allowing students to attend to their multiple identities and interests during their engineering and computing journeys. By recognizing the inherent value of multiple interests, practitioners encourage Latina students to bridge the gap between and leverage their multiple interests and engineering identities. While dismantling institutional silos may cause short-term challenges, the long-term benefits of investing in Latina students outweigh those challenges.

Once these structures are in place, practitioners should **encourage students to leverage multiple interests** during their engineering and computing journeys. Practitioners could look at how Latina students got interested in the fields in the first place or what topics excite them, as well as what their career goals are or what communities they want to serve with their talents. Rather than just telling students to leverage these interests, practitioners should take concrete steps to motivate Latina students to do so. Practitioners should look at ways in which students have built-in opportunities to leverage interests *within*, instead of adjacent to or outside of, their educational plan. This is particularly important for serving first-generation Latina college students, transfer students, or post-traditional students because they may be hesitant to deviate from traditional degree offerings.

Creating Interdisciplinary Relationships. To support the integration of multiple student interests, leaders should seek out opportunities to foster interdisciplinary relationships. Interdisciplinary relationships can take many forms but might look like **two or more disciplines coming together** to create experiences that encourage students to solve complex problems with a variety of viewpoints, tools, and understandings. These interdisciplinary relationships could be between disciplines within engineering and computing or between any disciplines on campus. Interdisciplinary relationships have the capacity to support Latina students in a variety of ways as they consider how to integrate their work in engineering and computing with other subjects.

For example, within engineering, these relationships might **come from interdisciplinary programs that bring together engineers of all kinds** to solve real-world problems given by companies. Although all the students might be engineers, each comes with a different perspective and set of possible tools to understand and solve the problem. This could mean mechanical engineers working with and learning from aerospace and software engineers or biomedical engineers collaborating with electrical and computer engineers.

In contrast, reaching out beyond engineering and computing, you might also seek interdisciplinary opportunities that **bring together seemingly disparate disciplines**, such as computing and ethics to design more ethical approaches to artificial intelligence, or computing and urban planning to optimize city services and public spaces. Computer science departments might also collaborate with cognitive scientists to work on projects related to human-computer interactions or partner with Spanish departments, Chicana/o/x studies, or women and gender studies to do more human-centered work.

Part of creating these interdisciplinary opportunities for engineering identity development for Latina engineering and computing students is building the relationships necessary for those programs to thrive. To do so, you might consider the following steps to **bring together like-minded individuals and incentivize interdisciplinary relationship building** over time. First, you need to find your "people"—the people who are also interested building interdisciplinary work on your campus or within your network. This might involve connecting with American Society for Engineering Education's (ASEE) Multidisciplinary Engineering Division or the Interdisciplinary Conference on Electrics and Computer (INTCEC). Second, you should consider the so-called wicked problems of engineering and computing—problems that are large, complex, and not easily solvable—as a place to discover which individuals on or off campus might be interested in interdisciplinary projects.

To incentivize faculty and staff to engage in this kind of relationship building, institutions might consider providing mini-grants or seed money, course buyouts, or shared equipment to faculty and staff who collaborate and involve students in interdisciplinary projects and coursework. Mini-grants or seed money could be used to build relationships and as a starting point to apply for greater funding opportunities in the future. Course buyouts could allow faculty the time and energy needed to connect across disciplines, and shared equipment could encourage multiple disciplines to work together on shared projects.

Think Beyond the Usual Partners

The quest to support engineering and computing identity requires us to know our students as well as look for areas of interest convergence. As such, practitioners should look for creative solutions to complex problems and think beyond their usual partners to gain a larger perspective of their institution outside of their own academic or organizational unit. While the usual partners, such as K–12 teachers, women's or multicultural centers, or STEM (science, technology, engineering, and mathematics) faculty, are inherently important to relationship building, practitioners could also look to less obvious, more creative partnerships.

Chicana feminism not only asks us to coalesce together on important issues and consider Latina students as complex but also emphasizes the need for more expansive thinking about what it means to become a Latina engineer. Thinking beyond the usual partners answers that call for more expansive thinking about how to meet students where they are and attend to the various identities that they hold. Your commitment to building relationships to foster creative solutions to complex problems can be thought of as an act of resistance against the tendency for our society to believe that there is one way of thinking or approaching problems.

Knowing Your Latina Engineering and Computing Students. It is entirely possible to get so caught up in the daily minutia of our positions that we forget or perhaps do not have adequate time **to pause and reflect on who our students are**. As I have mentioned previously, it is important to understand who you are serving; if you do not know who your Latina students are, it will be very difficult to build effective relationships in service to this population. Thinking beyond the usual partnerships means gaining a clear picture of who your Latina engineering and computing students are, what their needs and concerns are, and who or what organizations will best address those needs. For example, unusual partnerships might include those with interfaith initiatives (to address the intertwining of spirituality, religion, and engineering and computing) or advocacy and resources centers (to address the needs of low-income engineering and computing students).

Having a wider perspective enables you not only to have a clear understanding of the opportunities and constraints of your environment but also to be more creative in your approach to sustaining the engineering and computing interests of Latina students. While there are a variety of approaches to understanding one's student population, perhaps the best place to start is by **disaggregating data around retention and persistence**. Depending on the size of your Latina student population, you might consider looking at various identity markers, such as first-generation college students or low-income students, to get a better understand of their experiences.

Equity-minded practitioners might also **look to engagement surveys** to learn about the experiences of their Latina engineering and computing students. If available, National Survey of Student Engagement (NSSE) or Community College Survey of Student Engagement (CCSSE) results can both provide more information specifically about Latina student engagement and can be disaggregated by major. These surveys can provide insights on a variety of engagement factors, including academic and social experiences both in and outside of the classroom.

In addition to these activities, you might consider engaging in more qualitative approaches such as **listening sessions or focus groups** to better understand how Latina students are making sense of their engineering and computing experiences and identities. For example, you might ask students how they got interested in engineering or computing or when they most, or least, feel like an engineer or computer scientist. Likewise, you might consider asking about what other identities or experiences (e.g., anti-Blackness, low socioeconomic status, parental education) influence their engineering or computing identities or what supports they might like to see the institution create to support their identity development. Listening sessions or focus groups could be by discipline or field and form a basis for understanding the relationships you need to build to support Latina engineering and computing identity. What you hear may, or may not, surprise you. The important part here is understanding who you are serving and what partners are necessary.

Interest Convergence. Building these relationships, both with Latina students and with various partners, may require an acknowledgement of interest convergence over time. Interest convergence generally refers to when **two groups work toward a similar goal, often for very different and/or self-interested reasons**. Educational equity for racially and ethnically marginalized students is often fraught with pain points of interest convergence.[7] For example, one group may want to advocate for the engineering or computing identity needs of Latina students as a matter of social justice and equity, while another group merely supports this cause because they would like to enhance retention and persistence of these students in order to take their institution over the threshold to qualify as a Hispanic-serving institution (HSI) funding opportunities, with little care or attention to actually serving Latina students. While this kind of relationship building may feel inauthentic to many, these relationships are often ubiquitous in the higher education landscape. There are still benefits to these relationships and opportunities to demonstrate a commitment to students, even when relationships may seem peculiar or unlikely.

Thinking beyond the usual partners forces us to **find creative solutions to complex problems** around identity. While relationship building may be straightforward for some, you may also find yourself being forced to think outside the box. It may take continued investment, year after year, to get relationship building going, and along the way, you may have to expand how you define a partner or what relationship building looks like to meet the needs of Latina students and their complex identities. Overall, it is the persistent investment in these efforts that will bear fruit in the future, even if it is with the most unlikely of partners or relationship-building activities.

Reboot Representation

New York City, New York

When thinking about potential partners, you are wise *not* to forget the important role that organizations, like Reboot Representation, play in the ability to bring people together and strengthen collective impact. Reboot Representation is a coalition of leading tech companies that joined forces to double the number of Black, Latina, and Native American (BLNA) women receiving computing degrees by 2025. Their members collaborate in four major ways: (1) collective grantmaking; (2) speaking with a single voice about the issues facing BLNA women in computing; (3) preparing BLNA women computing undergraduates to enter tech careers; and (4) enabling industry partners to recruit, retain, and advance more BLNA women in tech. Reboot Representation coordinates among organizations with shared goals to pool resources, expertise, and networks. With over 1,200 members and 250 colleges and universities represented, they partner with tech companies to better understand how to provide resources to Latinas in the tech industry.

Callista Chen, the Senior Director of Programs at Reboot Representation, explained to me how the coalition funds research-backed projects that focus on recruiting BLNA women and girls and are implemented by nonprofit organizations (e.g., colleges and universities) with significant track records of serving these populations and are embedded within their communities. I particularly love their funding support of **Latinas de RTC (Rewriting the Code)**, which focuses on building community for Latinas pursuing computing degrees, including connecting them to other Latinas and celebrating Latina identity and heritage. Reboot Representation also supports Latina students in the **Computing Alliance of Hispanic-Serving Institutions (CAHSI) Student Scholars Program**, which helps CAHSI advance their mission and broaden success among Latina students, and Latina students at **Miami Dade College through their Women in Computing Initiative.** Unapologetically identity forward, this organization facilitates relationship-building practices that support various partners working together to develop computing identity for Latina students in ways that honor communities and promote inclusivity.

EXPANDING COMPETENCE AND PERFORMANCE THROUGH RELATIONSHIP BUILDING THAT IS DYNAMIC AND RESPONSIVE TO LATINA STUDENTS AND THEIR COMMUNITIES

While the task of expanding competence and performance has always been within the scope of higher education, utilizing relationship building that is dynamic and responsive to Latina students and their communities may be new, particularly within engineering and computing contexts. Within these fields important conversations persist about what knowledge and skills are needed within an ever-changing career landscape. Given the evolving nature of engineering and computing, the education Latina students receive must be dynamic and responsive to that landscape. No matter how landscapes shift, Latina students continue to face competence and performance experiences marked by sexism, racism, classism, and a whole host of other oppressions during identity development.[8]

Over the years, students in our studies took advantage of a range of services that supported competence and performance (e.g., tutoring, mentoring) and built their ways of knowing from a variety of sources, such as internships, family, mentors, and organizations.[9] However, they also articulated real challenges to their engineering identity, particularly around competence and performance.[10] Latina students were often stereotyped by their peers as incompetent and unable to perform engineering and computing tasks. They were often hesitant to ask questions for fear of making themselves vulnerable to the men around them and risking further marginalization. Latina students often found themselves separating their engineering and computing lives or being forced to obscure parts of their identities to be successful within these spaces. While they are resilient and may resist oppression, Latina students in engineering and computing deserve our attention to relationship building to support them in their competence and performance challenges.[11]

A Chicana feminist approach to expanding competence and performance would have us nurture relationships with Latina students and their communities, emphasizing the dynamic and responsive nature that is needed when meeting those community needs. Being dynamic means coming to the table with multiple creative ideas and having the energy to meet constant change. Being responsive means reacting to and answering the needs of Latina engineering and computing students and their communities, rather than imposing what *we* believe to be their needs. My recommendations for expanding competence and performance emphasize relationship building that is dynamic and responsive to Latina students. Within this section, I explore how to:

- **Address the real problems by:**
  - Preventing relationship building that is fundamentally deficit based
  - Having difficult conversations
  - Aligning the relationships, challenges, and strategies
- **Listen first and act second by:**
  - Understanding the issues and considering the impacts
  - Exercising intellectual humility
  - Trusting the process and being present
- **Respond to shifting issues by:**
  - Creating relationships that keep you informed and action oriented
  - Remaining grounded but open
  - Knowing when you need collaborators

Addressing the Real Problems

Almost everyone can agree that we need to enhance competence and performance in engineering and computing. Latina students in these fields have a responsibility to gain the knowledge and skills of their disciplines and function as an engineer or computer scientist who can apply those forms of learning. However, when we consider how to achieve that, we are not always focused on the *real* problems undergirding the work that we do. To expand competence and performance, we must make the most of our relationship building. For true identity building, you must be both innately aware of structural challenges and maintain an asset-based framework for addressing those challenges. It is through aligning relationships, challenges, and strategies that we maximize our ability to enhance engineering and computing identity in a dynamic and responsive way.

Preventing Relationship Building That Is Fundamentally Deficit Based. At times, we can all take a deficit-based perspective, and this is one of the main pitfalls I continue to see in relationship building and attention to Latina engineering and computing identity. It is only through reframing that we move our thinking and our **relationship building toward a more asset-based approach**. When one has a deficit-based perspective, that means one believes, whether implicitly or explicitly, that Latina students are lacking something, whether it be skills or experiences. Often cloaked in good intentions, deficit-based approaches often lead to relationship building that infantilizes Latina students or suggests practitioners know what is best for building their skills and activating their identity performances. This can undergird the relationships that we form and initiatives that we support, which has implications for how we serve Latina students in these fields.

Although there is certainly value in expertise, deficit-based approaches ignore the vast community cultural wealth and funds of identity that Latina students bring with them to their fields.[12] **Latina students bring knowledge from their families and communities** that informs what they know about the world of engineering and computing, even if they do not have family members who work directly as engineers or computer scientists. For example, students may possess geographical knowledge that they have picked up from living in rural communities with their families that could be foundational for designing infrastructure in underdeveloped areas. Ignoring these forms of wealth permeates the relationships that we build and how our work is approached. Using an asset-based approach—building on those forms of wealth—can encourage better and more impactful relationship building with community partners, particularly those from Latinx backgrounds or who serve this community.

To combat deficit-based approaches, particularly in newly formed relationships, you might consider **leading teams in an asset map-building exercise** in which you highlight assets of Latina engineering and computing students and possible on- and off-campus resources that might be leveraged for identity building. For example, you might encourage your team members to consider the assets that they have seen students bring with them to their experience, such as resilience in the face of difficult obstacles or strong familial ties that support their success, as well as identify assets on campus, such as a multicultural center or strong Society of Hispanic Professional Engineers (SHPE) organization, that might be potential partners. Fundamentally, this exercise is meant to keep the conversations and vision setting as asset based in nature and to remind team members that it is the system they are seeking to reform, rather than the individual student.

Having Difficult Conversations. Addressing real problems for Latina engineering and computing identity development pushes us to consider what forms of privilege and oppression are at play within the context of our relationship-building efforts. You and your collaborators must **reckon with the idea that if Latina students in engineering and computing are oppressed that there** must **be an oppressor**. Even equity-minded practitioners may be reluctant to embrace a critical perspective. For many, the acknowledgement of oppressions can be easy, but the acknowledgement of the oppressor—and sometimes our own complicity in that oppression—is at times difficult to face or share with our partners.

Talking about sexism or racism may come naturally in discussions around equity and identity. However, it is far harder to admit—especially if you are Latin* yourself—that you may perpetuate anti-Blackness or Indigenous erasure in your work with Latina students. **You may be the problem, indeed. We all are at some point or another.** However, it is not an admission of permanent failure to admit you are the problem. It can be liberating, normal, and necessary to be self-critical and move beyond performativity to real support of Latina students. Likewise, it may be difficult to articulate to your partners how their otherwise lovely professional formation activities (e.g., career preparation, interviewing skills) might perpetuate forms of toxic masculinity and performative whiteness against Latina students.

It can be a challenging conversation to say that members of the faculty, staff, and student body are, in effect, the oppressors. These are not comfortable conversations to have over coffee. Nor are these conversations that come naturally in the course of relationship building. Yet to build a sense of trust and rapport, they are essential. To **gain more confidence in engaging** in these types of conversations, it might be helpful to read the following texts: *Difficult Conversations: How to Discuss What Matters Most* or *Crucial Conversations: Tools for Talking When Stakes Are High.*[13] Both of these texts address how to avoid defensiveness, communicate more effectively, and move toward better problem-solving. In thinking about engineering and computing identity for Latina students, you must become clear and focused on the fundamental issues affecting students and learn how to handle difficult conversations. Difficult conversations might include unpacking the reasons behind student outcomes or breaking down how our institutions place roadblocks in the pathways of engineering and computing students.

Aligning the Relationships, Challenges, and Strategies. To address the real or perceived challenges associated with engineering and computing identity development, it is imperative that **practitioners align their relationships, challenges, and strategies.** It is impossible to affect real change for Latina students without ensuring that you have a clear understanding of what the actual problem is, what strategies are available to solve it, and who needs to be involved. You can have the right relationships built and understand the challenges, but if you have selected the wrong strategy, your efforts will be inefficient or even harmful. Similarly, you can inherently know the challenges that Latina students face and have an idea of the strategies to address identity, but without sufficient sustained partnerships, these efforts run the risk of relying on a single equity champion or being limited in their ability to meet the needs of students. Beyond the existence of these connections, the alignment between each of these elements is essential to an institution's ability to be dynamic and responsive to students' needs; if the methods are not tailored, change will not happen.

One exercise that teams can take to ensure that they are aligning relationships, challenges, and strategies for enhancing Latina student engineering and computing identity is to **create a logic model**. Logic models can help teams articulate a common goal and identify relevant inputs, outputs, external influences, and outcomes. For example, if your team was interested in building engineering or computing identity for Latina students as a main goal, you might consider the demographics or typical experiences of the Latina population at your institution and the available initiatives and resources. For example, are students often working and balancing family responsibilities? What are the challenges here? Next, you might consider what activities and groups you might like to focus on, such as Latina student mentoring, interdisciplinary peer-based teams, or faculty workshops. Then, consider your outcomes, including short- and long-term goals, and how you will measure them. In looking at the logic model, step back and ask yourselves whether all the pieces align. The relationships, challenges, and strategies for engineering and computing identity must all align; otherwise, your team will not meet their goal as effectively as possible. Every effort should be made to consider what relationship building and conversations need to take place in order to more fully align these pieces before actions are taken.

Rutgers University

Garden State Louis Stokes Alliance for Minority Participation (LSAMP), Newark, New Jersey

I will admit that I am biased when it comes to LSAMP programs. Since their inception in the early 1990s, in so many places, with so many students, LSAMP programs across the nation are doing the work of aligning relationships, challenges, and strategies. Named in honor of former Congressman Louis Stokes, the first African American Ohio congressman, LSAMP programs have the clear and audacious goals of leveraging partnerships to increase STEM degrees of underrepresented populations and supporting research on STEM participation and program impacts.

New Jersey is home to a large, diverse, and continuously growing Latin* population, and initiatives such as the LSAMP have responded to growing the STEM talent of Latin* students. The Garden State LSAMP (GS-LSAMP) is an alliance of seven New Jersey universities and one community college aimed at supporting STEM student success for racially and ethnically marginalized students. GS-LSAMP partners include Essex County College, Fairleigh Dickinson, Kean, Montclair State, New Jersey Institute of Technology, Rutgers (New Brunswick and Newark), and William Paterson. GS-LSAMP provides academic support, specialized advising, mentoring, and paid research opportunities with university faculty. Students also participate in a learning community, receive stipends for various activities (e.g., tutoring, leading study groups, community service), and attend and present their own research at the annual GS-LSAMP conference. To enhance the pathway for STEM students, GS-LSAMP offers connections to two other programs, the Northern New Jersey Bridges to Baccalaureate (NNJ-B2B), which supports community college student transfer, and the Bridge to the Doctorate (B2D) program, which supports the transition to graduate school. The NNJ-B2B brings together associate degree–granting HSIs committed to improving STEM degree transfer for students from Latin* and other racially and ethnically marginalized backgrounds. NJ-B2B partners include Passaic County Community College, Hudson County Community College, County College of Morris, and Union County College. The NNJ-B2B provides financial (e.g., $32,000 plus two years of tuition) and academic support (e.g., mentoring, professional development, research, faculty/staff support) to cohorts of graduate students.

GS-LSAMP executive director, Dr. Alec Gates, a professor of earth and environmental science at Rutgers University, credits the success of these initiatives to the team's desire to create a visual pathway for students in which they can see others who look like them engaged in the kind of work that they want to do. They also have a commitment to "try anything" and be responsive to the needs, identities, and backgrounds of the students they serve, which has served them well as they adapt to the changing needs of students. Although these programs are not exclusively focused on Latina students, they do serve as models for promising practices seeking to connect Latina students, particularly those from HSIs and/or community colleges, to engineering and computing opportunities at four-year institutions in ways that leverage relationship building and structural supports.

Listening First, Acting Second

I am impatient by nature. I want things done yesterday, and the slow machination of higher education change and investment by institutions sometimes frustrates me. For many of us, the act of listening first and then, after careful consideration, acting is an exercise in both patience and keeping our wits about us. However, when it comes to relationship building and constructing experiences for engineering and computing identity, learning to listen first and act second is necessary to lay a foundation of truly understanding the issues at hand, exercising intellectual humility, and trusting in the process. Attending to each of these elements ensures that we are not hasty in our desire to build out competence and performance at the expense of our relationship building. Likewise, meaningful relationship building is more likely to take place when we approach the process with a sense of care and reverence.

Understanding the Issues and Considering the Impacts. Listening first and then acting gives us the opportunity to understand the issues and consider the impacts of the relationships we build. Although any team can address competence and performance issues for Latina students, it is the team that has thoroughly **understood the context and preexisting landscape** that stands the best chance of meaningful impact. This looks like making a concerted effort to get to know potential partners, investing time and energy to educate yourself on the local context, and discovering what strategies have been used in the past. In addition, learning what the values and expectations of those relationships are can clarify not only the context for identity but also the leverage points for buy-in across stakeholders.

Leadership and Diversity Scholarships

Oregon Tech, Klamath Falls, Oregon

Known for its engineering, technology, and applied sciences programs, Oregon Tech has created identity-forward supportive structures through their **Leadership and Diversity (LAD) scholarships**. LAD scholarship recipients receive three thousand to four thousand dollars to support their education. Many considerations are made in selecting students, including their background, identities, and what they might bring to the Oregon Tech community. Although open to all students, given the makeup of Oregon Tech, many scholarship recipients are engineering and computing students from minoritized backgrounds and, increasingly, from Latin* communities. **Thomas Arce, former director of student involvement and belonging at Oregon Tech**, explained that students, many of whom are in engineering and computing, attend events on social identity development, leadership, and cultural competency as well as meet with a staff member from the Student Involvement and Belonging Department once per term. Scholarship recipients also engage with a common read, the latest focused on incorporating social identity and leadership development, and have the opportunity to connect with industry partners through collaborations with the Society for Women Engineers (SWE).

While the scholarship has been around for many years, the identity-forward aspects of the program came in response to NSSE findings that showed that Oregon Tech students scored below average on students reflecting on their cultural identity and skills for engaging in cross-cultural dialogue. To meet this need, program leaders at this predominantly white institution decided to revolutionize how they implemented leadership programming for scholarship recipients, and a new version of LAD was born. I particularly appreciate that LAD represents an approach for how institutions can create identity-forward support structures that blend identity, culture, and leadership to support Latina engineering and computing students. And perhaps most importantly, LAD also represents an example of how institutions can listen before acting in order to truly understand the issues that their students are facing and consider how to shift their actions accordingly.

Exercising Intellectual Humility. I often find myself in rooms of experts: technical experts, educational experts, policy experts, community-based organizing experts, people with engineering and computing expertise and others with higher education expertise, people with law or leadership backgrounds, as well as historians, ethnic studies theorists, and the like. So. Many. Experts. It can be fascinating to watch individuals flex their expertise—like watching a solo cellist or a professional athlete shine—but it can also be painful to see colleagues posturing and insisting that their approach is the only approach. I once sat in a meeting with an engineering colleague during which this person asserted that there were no experts who studied engineering education concepts for marginalized college students. They wished for someone who understood the engineering identity process. I had been on their project team for at least six months, and yet they had no idea that I was indeed *that person*. Relationship building in these moments can feel exasperating and uncertain, even when you have the best of partners. In these cases, a bit of intellectual humility might best serve the relationship-building process.

Intellectual humility has us **acknowledge our own limitations** in understanding how to approach building competence and performance opportunities for Latina students, and it allows us to push toward our goals from a standpoint of seeking truth and understanding. This may be particularly important as you build relationships with practitioners of color who may have expertise and experiences with Latina students who can greatly inform the work that you do together. To exercise intellectual humility for projects on Latina students in engineering and computing education, you might consider how you can continue to **keep an open mind** to the subject, even if you feel passionately about the topic, and continue to ask questions with the true intention of growing your understanding. You might *not* have the needed expertise, but someone on your team or at your institution might. Bringing them into the conversation demonstrates intellectual humility and commitment to the work. Also, **examine your assumptions** for elements of bias and ways of thinking that might be outdated or not serving you. Intellectual humility can guide you to better relationships in your collaborations and a more open approach to solving problems as they arise in creating support structures for Latina students in engineering and computing.

Trusting the Process and Being Present. To expand competence and performance, relationships must develop. Trust that the process is one of **inevitable change** and that relationship building is one of many seasons. You may have to go through several iterations of what partners you connect with and how you choose to engage with the work. These iterations may see a reshuffling of priorities, difficult conversations about the goal, and even letting go of potential partners. The situation that you are facing may look dark now, but through relationship building, you and your team can make it better. As equity-minded practitioners, it is your responsibility to continue to trust the process of change and be **fully present to the good work** that is happening. If you stay in the game, you will see relationships develop and engineering identity enhanced for Latina students.

Trusting the process and being present means taking meaningful steps to **connect with your partners** when you meet with them. Turn off your phone, close your laptop, and avoid multitasking—tall orders in today's busy world—to express your gratitude for their time and energy and your willingness to fully engage. Take time to meet in person, if at all possible. Although Zoom is great for bridging distances and keeping people connected, it cannot replace the synergy that happens when people are in the same room together. Whether it means coming together regularly for your on-campus partners or annually for your off-campus partners, build these activities into your plans and budgets.

Entrust your partners to take actions to continue nurturing your alliance and support Latina student identity. While there may be additional conversation around the choices that are made and how to improve services, initiatives, and priorities, being with your partners on this relationship-building journey allows you to be responsive and dynamic in your overall strategy. The most effective projects that I have ever been a part of were ones in which my colleagues trusted my expertise and judgment. This is not to say that they did not push back on decisions or ask questions about rationale, but in general, they trusted my expertise and allowed me to do my piece, I trusted them to do theirs, and we met together to see how we could bring those pieces together. To fully serve the identity development of Latina students, you must consider how you will leverage the expertise of team members and build in regular checkpoints to ensure that the relationship is continuing to flourish as well as the initiative. Finally, beyond this, you should also be **flexible and have grace** with your partners as you all learn how to best move within these relationships. Being flexible and having grace within relationship building means being responsive to the needs of your team and being willing to work through any issues that arise, without threats to dissolution of the relationship itself.

Issues Shift and So Must You, Shape-Shifter

Throughout Gloria Anzaldúa's works, she uses shape-shifting imagery to allude to the deep, transformative, and often spiritual inner work that takes place around identity development.[14] We can draw inspiration from her belief that identity "is a changing cluster of components and a shape-shifting activity."[15] While some may associate shape-shifting with the dark intentions of dishonesty or morally bankrupt charlatans, Anzaldúa's viewpoint suggests that shape-shifting is an asset in which one's identities, ideas, and actions are fluid and responsive and can evolve over time. It is the path of *conocimientos*, the path of understanding and knowing. There is a certain, almost spiritual power in the ability to expand one's understanding, move in many directions, and transform at will.

Similarly, practitioners must also shape-shift. Shape-shifting is a transformation from one form to the next, whether it be subtle or complete, quick or over time. It emphasizes a dynamic rather than static approach to identity and the way that we do our work. This type of shape-shifting allows practitioners to stand in the power of our own expertise and ways of knowing while also creating relationships that will keep us informed, action oriented, and open to new possibilities.

Creating Relationships That Keep You Informed and Action Oriented. The act of creating relationships that keep you informed and action oriented is an early step toward shape-shifting on your path to *conocimientos* (understanding) engineering and computing identity for Latina students. To enhance student competence and performance and be responsive to the needs of students and their communities, we must build and sustain good connections. It is essential that we work with our **K–12 partners**. Too often, higher education practitioners lay blame on K–12 settings for sending them students whom they deem "underprepared" without meaningfully engaging individuals in those settings about how they can cocreate meaningful engineering and computing pathways. We must work with our K–12 partners to understand the challenges present in those educational settings, including an understanding of the implications of standardized testing and other legislative mandates that K–12 partners face.

Practitioners should also consider how improving relationship building between **community college and four-year institutions** could provide a solid foundation for growing and supporting engineering and computing competence and performance for Latina students. For example, you could solidify articulation agreements between partner institutions and enhance transfer course offerings to provide the most comprehensive and smooth educational journey for Latina engineering and computing students. It could also mean improving alignment between community colleges and four-year institutions; leaders should enhance transfer course offerings. Throughout these conversations, leaders should consider striving for a balance of power between institutions and ensure that all leaders and the students they represent feel a sense of efficacy and voice in the process.

Practitioners should also consider sustained relationships with **industry partners** who care about the success and identity development of Latina engineering and computing students. For example, institutions can support Latina engineering and computing students by giving them more frequent and meaningful interactions with industry partners, whereas over time, companies can develop relationships with these students to recruit top talent. Sustained relationships allow these students to have access to great opportunities for engineering and computing identity performances, not just near graduation but across the college journey.

Finally, practitioners should consider establishing **research to practice (and vice versa) relationships** to make research-informed decisions. These relationships also ensure that scholars stay grounded in their research and get feedback about how their recommendations are (or are not) working in real-world settings. As a scholar myself, I can say that these relationships have been among the most fulfilling—and challenging—spaces that I have ever occupied, but I can also say without a doubt that they have strengthened my resolve to do the work and have continuously increased my admiration for the leaders of today who are faced with a litany of challenges.

University of Texas at El Paso

Computing Alliance of Hispanic-Serving Institutions, El Paso, Texas

In terms of creating relationships that keep you informed and action oriented, look no further than the **Computing Alliance of Hispanic-Serving Institutions (CAHSI)** at the University of Texas, El Paso (UTEP). For almost twenty years, CAHSI has been committed to growing and sustaining a strong network of individuals and groups across the country committed to the recruitment, retention, and acceleration of Latin* students and professionals in computing. CAHSI is made up of both four-year and two-year HSIs, STEM alliances, industry leaders, nonprofits, and government entities working toward collective impact. Partners include Microsoft, Google, AnitaB.org, CSforAll, and Lockheed Martin, among many others. CAHSI focuses on research that looks at organizational behavior or HSIs that advance Latin* success and effective academic support structures and culturally relevant strategies. CAHSI is also highly involved in capacity building and organizing networks and collaborations that seek to enhance and diversify the computing workforce. The organization works to build relationships and capacity at the institutional and individual levels, the alliance and regional levels, and the national level and has been nationally recognized by the White House Initiative on Educational Excellence for Hispanics and by *Excelencia* in Education in its Growing What Works database.

Dr. Ann Quiroz Gates, whose work I admire so much that I asked her to write the foreword for this book, serves as the Senior Advisor to the Provost on Strategic STEM Initiatives and Executive Director of CAHSI at UTEP. Over the years, Dr. Gates has emphasized the importance of breaking down barriers for Latin* students to enter and be successful in computing and encouraged institutions to move away from silos that inhibit progress addressing challenges within computing. Through her work with CAHSI, she has made a commitment to changing the demographics of

Latin* students in computing and ensuring that there are a range of different voices at the table to address these issues. What I love about CAHSI is its ability to facilitate relationship building among a variety of stakeholders at multiple levels in order to discuss and take action on creating more equitable structures for computing students at HSIs. These relationships have been the catalyst for helping countless Latina computing students enter and be successful within HSI settings and allowed them to do so in spaces that are more culturally relevant and attentive to their needs than ever before.

Remaining Grounded but Open. The call for shape-shifting is not without difficulty. If they don't stay grounded, equity-minded practitioners run the risk of drifting into existential dread, overwork, or a diffusion of action and meaning. Although it is important to remain open to possibilities and shifts in perspective, it is essential to **remember why you are building relationships and who you are serving**. In particular, the desire to serve Latina students within engineering and computing can become fraught with a host of challenges as one battles not only the patriarchy and systemic racism but also potentially a whole host of other oppressions, feelings, and personalities in the relationship-building mix. A sense of being grounded will allow you to weather the inevitable ups and downs of relationship building and the complications that come with interpersonal interactions and organizational systems.

Knowing When You Need Collaborators. Enhancing competence and performance experiences for Latina engineering and computing students is no small feat. Couple that with trying to be identity forward in your strategies and taking a Chicana feminist, asset-based approach, and you have a recipe for exhaustion and potential burnout. You cannot do it alone, nor should you. There comes a time when you realize that you need collaborators. **Collaborators and relationships are not only needed to build and sustain the work but also essential for you to grow and remain steady.** While we all know that person who continuously works alone as a champion, giving themselves to an all-consuming albeit amazing project, I cannot help but wonder at what cost this comes not only to the individual but also to the institution and the students whom they serve. Without relationships and collaborators, practitioners risk their efforts falling apart.

INTENSIFYING RECOGNITION OPPORTUNITIES THROUGH CREATING RELATIONSHIPS THAT RESPECT HISTORY, CULTURE, AND LATINA WAYS OF KNOWING

Each day, Latina students engage in a series of moments in which they recognize or dismiss their identities as engineers and computer scientists. Although all aspects of engineering and computing identity are essential, it is imperative that Latina students see themselves in these roles. These issues influence how Latina students choose to enter engineering and computing fields, how they persist, and where they see themselves after graduation.[16]

Self-recognition is an acknowledgment of one's skills and performances and the ability to see oneself as a part of these fields. Outside recognition refers to how other people recognize those skills, validate identity performances, and see one as a future member of the field. Latina students, due to a variety of experiences and oppressions, often do not see themselves as the kinds of people who "do" engineering or computing.[17] And when they do manage to see themselves in these roles, there may be others in their lives who dismiss their sense of identity. The ability of Latina students to see themselves as engineers and computer scientists is a complicated phenomenon wrapped up in issues ranging from whiteness, racialization, and an erasure of indigeneity to microaggressions and sexism.[18]

Although identity recognition is often thought of as an individual act that primarily concerns one's individual cognition and how one makes meaning of one's own experiences, our findings highlight the innate nature of seeing oneself in these roles as a social experience that could be enhanced through relationship building and an antioppressive approach to who an engineer or computer scientist should be. To take this approach, you must honor, but not essentialize, students' histories, cultures, and Latina ways of knowing as well as support the shared values, beliefs, and practices derived from the Latin* community that will support Latina students in recognizing themselves as engineers and computer scientists.

Rooted in Chicana feminism, Gilberto Conchas and Nancy Acevedo's book entitled *The Chicana/o/x Dream: Hope, Resistance and Educational Success* encourages us to see that "students navigate higher education systems successfully as individuals whose hope and resistance results in successfully building bridges between higher education and their communities."[19] The imagery of bridges hearkens back to many other Chicana feminist texts in which the building of bridges is meant to be a transformative approach to understanding oneself, situating oneself within the world, and coalition building. As *nepantleras*, you are the ones who build bridges for our students. My recommendations for intensifying recognition opportunities focus on creating relationships that respect history, culture, and Latina ways of knowing. In this section, I explore how to:

- **Immerse yourself in the Chicano Movement and an ethos of Chicana feminism by:**
  - Recognizing the rich scholarly, activist, and community-based wealth of knowledge and strengths surrounding Latina students
  - Learning lessons from the Chicano Movement
  - Creating an ethos of Chicana feminism
- **Blur the lines between the institution and Latin* communities by:**
  - Rejecting "subtractive schooling" and assimilationist relationships
  - Welcoming in *la familia*, not just for outreach
  - Being okay with being uncomfortable
- **Question who we are asking Latina students to become by:**
  - Focusing on recognition and value signaling
  - Reframing who we think of as meaningful identity actors
  - Stopping the perpetuation of trauma

Immersing Yourself in the Chicano Movement and an Ethos of Chicana Feminism

Although you may not be a Chicano/a/* studies scholar, or even a feminist scholar, there is value in immersing yourself in an understanding of the Chicano Movement and an ethos of Chicana feminism. Doing so can provide you with insight about the history, culture, and educational experiences of Latina students in the United States and an understanding of the need for Chicana feminism within engineering and computing identity work.

Recognizing the Rich Scholarly, Activist, and Community-Based Wealth of Knowledge and Strengths Surrounding Latina Students. We must begin to uncover and honor the rich scholarly, activist, and community-based wealth of knowledge and strengths. We do this by understanding and putting into practice within our relationship building the **history and inherent value that**

Latin* communities have and how that serves as a strong foundation for Latina students as they build their engineering and computing identities. Our relationship building only becomes enhanced when we begin to see that we, even those who do not identify as Latin*, play a part in a much larger and historical movement toward equity for Latina students and their communities. We truly **stand on the shoulders of giants**—those who came before us and problematized these issues—and it is from those scholars, activists, and community members that we can derive strength and fortitude to continue despite obstacles.

Lessons from the Chicano Movement. You do not have to be a historian to recognize how integral the Chicano Movement was and is for Latin* students in this country. **Its legacy of supporting Latin* educational equity continues today.** The rights to fair labor practices, equal housing, and equitable educational outcomes are all legacies from the movement, without which our community would have been deeply marginalized. From nationally visible figures such as César Chávez and Dolores Huerta to dedicated local organizations such as University of Texas, Austin's Mexican American Student Organization (MASO) and Mexican American Youth Organization (MAYO), the effects of the Chicano Movement's work continue to be felt (and challenged) today. These individuals and groups sought to eliminate inequities for Latin* communities and create educational systems that acknowledge the histories and cultures of the community. By contextualizing our engineering and computing efforts within this movement, we shift our efforts from seeming discreet to being **part of a much larger, sustained movement for equity**.

An Ethos of Chicana Feminism. Like all movements, the Chicano Movement was not without its flaws. Entrenched with misogyny and sexism as well as colorism and homophobia, the civil rights movement, the Chicano Movement, and Latin* communities often had little tolerance for individuals who did not look, act, or think similarly to those with power. Chicana feminism rose out of these marginalizations—out of **a desire to no longer be on the sidelines of movements** or society, a declaration of individuals as complex human beings with **many facets to their identities and experiences**. It is from this place that we can embody an ethos of Chicana feminism within the work that we do to enhance Latina engineering and computing identity. Acknowledging these complexities and refuting the othering of members of our community lay an important foundation not only for understanding issues of identity recognition but also for relationship building to further these initiatives. We have a responsibility to hold ourselves, as well as our partners, to a higher standard.

Blurring the Lines Between the Institution and Latin* Communities

So often, higher education is accused, either fairly or unfairly, of sitting atop the ivory tower, enforcing distance between ourselves and the community. It is only through our relationship building with Latin* communities that meaningful work can be done. The desire to create more affirming moments for engineering and computing identity recognition is intertwined with the ability of practitioners to remove the barriers between the institution and Latin* communities.

Not "Subtractive Schooling," Not Assimilationist Relationships. As a young scholar, I took every opportunity to build relationships, sometimes pairing up with individuals who may or may not have shared my views of the need to honor the community cultural wealth of Latin* communities. Over time, I have learned to anchor STEM project relationship building by focusing on two elements: that we honor communities and that we do not ask students to assimilate. I am inspired by the work of scholars like Angela Valenzuela, a University of Texas, Austin professor, whose work with Latin* communities I have long admired, to ensure that I oppose all elements of "subtractive schooling" that devalue Latin* cultures and languages.[20]

Likewise, I am inspired by Ebony McGee's work to resist white supremacy and assimilationist tactics that often pervade our understandings of students' experiences and resulting STEM equity efforts.[21] Taken together, these concepts point toward the need for relationship building that is foundationally asset based in its incorporation of Latin* ways of knowing and being. Rather than asking Latina students to leave their identities and communities at the proverbial door in favor of an identity-evasive approach to engineering and computing, we should **build partnerships that encourage students to bring their full selves** to their educational experiences. Equity-minded practitioners should examine their approaches to identity recognition for **hidden biases, assumptions, and values that are rooted in masculine norms and white supremacy** (e.g., individualism, paternalism, either/or thinking, objectivity).[22]

Welcoming in* La Familia*, and Not Just for Outreach. Blurring the lines between the institution and Latin* communities means welcoming in *la familia*—and by *la familia*, I am not talking about merely immediate or even extended family. I refer to the greater *familia* of Latin* peoples who make up the communities around us. They are the grandmothers, brothers, activists, clergy, and children who make these communities who they are. And while higher education institutions have made great strides in welcoming families to campus (e.g., family days, family organizations, parent involvement offices), these invitations to the family and community are often limited to the outreach or graduation phases of the educational journey, as if students did not need clear connections to the community throughout their journey. Furthermore, the invitation is just that—an invitation—extended on behalf of the institution *to* families and the community. The *institution* dictates the terms by which Latin* families and communities are welcomed on campus. Even when families and communities are invited on campus, it may often be for general events rather than events that explicitly build relationships with engineering and computing.

Victoria

When Bringing Your Full Self and Familia *to Engineering Becomes Complicated*

Sometimes institutions make it difficult for Latina students to bring their full selves to the engineering context. Other times, institutions are not welcoming to families. And in some cases, it is both. Victoria, an engineering major at a large predominantly white institution, by all accounts was your typical student. She had a rigorous course schedule, was close friends with other women in engineering, and worried about graduate school possibilities. She had initially struggled in engineering but eventually found her groove working in a research group with a woman principal investigator (PI) who she respected and felt supported by. However, Victoria had an entire part of her life that she kept obscured from peers, faculty, and her university community. Hundreds of miles away, she had a daughter who was quietly being raised by her family so that she could attend one of the most prestigious universities in the nation. A teen mother, she had made the difficult decision to leave her family, community, and baby behind so that she could attend the state's flagship institution and position herself for graduate school and better career opportunities. Even at a young age,

Victoria had a strong engineering identity and was committed to seeing her dreams come true. Her parents believed in her and were willing to support her through this decision and provide a nurturing home for her child. She kept all this a secret from her university community because she feared ostracization by her peers and felt as though faculty and staff would treat her differently based on her circumstances. She felt as though it was very difficult for others to recognize her as both a mother *and* an engineer and that her family would not be welcome on campus. For years, she did not disclose this information to her PI and kept her life divided. As Victoria approached graduation, she reconciled her engineering identity with her identity as a mother and part of a Latin* family. She ultimately attended graduate school and is now gainfully employed within her field. Although she held a strong engineering identity and was ultimately successful, it begs the question of what might have been different had she felt able to bring her full self to the university environment.

This represents a missed opportunity to **leverage the wealth of families and communities** for instilling a sense of recognition for Latina students. Through enhanced relationship building with these groups, Latina students can experience a stronger connection between the worlds that they come from and the careers that they have chosen. Picture this, a Latina student whose engineering identity has been influenced by her family and local community decides that she wants to pursue this field to address water infrastructure issues in Latin America. Her institution welcomes and celebrates not only her interests but also those who made those interests possible. Her **family is welcomed** into the college of engineering before she even starts college and is invited back every year for various robotics and STEM days and for her interdisciplinary capstone project that allowed her to leverage her Spanish linguistic capital and her family's knowledge of working with Latin American water systems. Her family beams with pride as *mija* presents her work, and they are elated when she becomes the first in her family to earn an engineering degree upon graduation. Being involved with the college of engineering has become such an ingrained piece of their family's experience that they send two more children to the campus. This is the dream.

New Mexico State University

Young Women in Computing, Las Cruces, New Mexico

For almost twenty years, the **Young Women in Computing (YWiC) program at New Mexico State University (NMSU)** has worked toward enhancing the enrollment and graduation of women in computer science. When the program started, the university's enrollment in computer science was half of the national average, but now, NMSU is one of nation's top producers of women in the field. Over the years, the program has served over twenty-five thousand students, many of whom, based on the location and significant presence of Latin* communities, are Latina. YWiC serves a range of ages, including elementary, middle, and high schoolers, as they prepare for their pathways to higher education. In preparation to enter college, high school girls are exposed to YWiC curriculum that includes topics such as LilyPad Arduino, Python, LiveCode, and cybersecurity and encryption.

Dr. Enrico Pontelli, founder of YWiC, dean of the College of Arts and Sciences, and a Regents professor of computer science at NMSU, explained to me that the secret behind their success has been learning from their failures, allowing students to take a leadership role, and consistently showing up for families over time. Dr. Pontelli related that the first time they did work in this area it did not work because the students, many of whom were women of color, were not connecting with the mostly white male instructors. It was only when they allowed women undergraduate students to lead that they started seeing results. YWiC participants began connecting with the women undergraduate students and enjoying the camps much more. It was also a win because YWiC participants felt more comfortable expressing their experiences in computing with the program's women undergraduates, allowing for close bonds to be created and an avenue for the team's leaders to receive feedback to make adjustments to the program as needed. Over time, YWiC activities have become something that Latin* families anticipate, trust, and value due to the program's consistency over time and responsiveness to familial and community needs. This has meant hiring Spanish-speaking team members and holding family nights to get families involved in the computing education process. What I love about YWiC is that it creates a clear pathway for Latina students to see themselves as the kind of people who do computing. The initiative builds in opportunities for skill development and continues to update its curriculum to meet the varying computing interests that students have. I also appreciate the work that the program has done to attend to the multiple identities and backgrounds that students bring with them (e.g., language, gender, migrant families) and that it is willing to reassemble programming and curriculum as needed in order to meet the computing identity development needs of its participants. Furthermore, the program's commitment to families and communities demonstrates a clear dedication to honoring the valuable community cultural wealth that exists in Las Cruces and the desire to remain connected with local communities.

Being Okay with Being Uncomfortable. Finally, it is not possible to remove the barriers between institutions and Latin* communities without **being okay with being uncomfortable**. Although it may seem awkward at first to build these relationships with an eye toward engineering and computing identity, it will get easier. Relationship building with Latin* communities takes time, as does gaining trust, particularly because many in the community may be suspicious of higher education's motives, values, and intentions for their student. There may be **hard questions, flared tempers, and ups and downs**, but the benefits outweigh the associated risks if you can just sit in that discomfort and continue to express your commitment and demonstrated support for Latin* students and their engineering and computing identity.

Who Are We Asking Latina Students to Become?

Every time I interview a Latina student, I think about this question. The answer is not simple. On one hand, there are many institutions that ask Latina students to integrate their various identities, cultures, and values into the work that they do to become recognized as engineers or computer scientists who can bring their full selves into their careers. In this example, they are empowered to be who they are, can move within these fields as proud Latina women possessing multiple identities, and are driven by strong curiosity for the subject and an innate desire to problem solve and design. On the other hand, there are just as many institutions that ask Latina students to check their identities at the door and assimilate to what others believe an engineer or computer scientist should look and act like. In this example, Latina students remain tethered to deficit models that portray them as not good enough or lacking and often allow institutions to define their engineering identities for them. In such cases, these Latina students are pushed, pulled, and molded into a version of themselves that they may not even recognize by the time that they complete their degrees, should they choose to remain in the field at all. To prevent this from happening, we must ask ourselves again: Who are we asking Latina students to become if they are to be successful within engineering and computing? How do we create opportunities for Latina students to find their place within these fields? And how can we tailor identity recognition experiences that honor history, culture, and Latina ways of knowing while liberating Latina students to pursue these fields in ways that are both authentic to them and free from imposed trauma?

Ashley

Finding One's Place in the World of Computing Is a Process of Becoming

Who we ask Latina students to become during the course of their studies matters. How we structure coursework, who we hire, and what their interests are matter. The kinds of careers that we expose our students to matter. For example, Ashley studied computing at a large, public, predominantly white institution. She was active in her diversity in computing student organization and closely connected to her department and academic advisors. She excelled in her technical courses and was undeterred by her status as what she calls a "double minority" as a Latina woman in computing spaces, often taking the lead on outreach activities and mentoring peers to support their success. By all accounts, she was flourishing as a student, both in and outside of the classroom. However, she felt a fundamental misalignment between her program and her career prospects, values, and commitment to her community. Although her program ranks among the top ten in the nation, she felt as though her program did not seek to solve real-world, meaningful problems. She believed that her program and its faculty and students were only interested in the latest tech and making apps and that solutions for communities and challenges like clean water went unmentioned.

She lamented the missed opportunities for her to apply her technical skills and revealed a feeling of isolation, even though she was highly involved in computing activities. She wished she could invest her time and energy into something meaningful with real-world impact, rather than just profit margins for corporations. She felt as though her transition into the workforce would mean sacrificing her values and dreams to be employable, given the industry partners that she was being groomed for by her department. Growing up in one of the most impoverished regions in the United States, her view of the purpose and potential of computing was intertwined with her desire to serve her community and the world with her talents as best she could. However, going back to her region or even serving a different community felt out of reach for her given the current expectations. And although she felt as though her computing identity was strong—she loved every aspect of the work—she was unsure about who her program was asking her to become and where it might take her in the future.

Recognition and Value Signaling. The recognition that we bestow upon students signals our implicit values and what we think of as the ideal engineer or computer scientist. If we recognize students for their abilities to self-sacrifice, work themselves to death, and estrange themselves from their families and communities, that says something about our values. If we recognize students for their ability to transform themselves into the kind of person *we* think an engineer should look like, this also says something about our values. Part of interrogating how we recognize Latina students as engineers and computer scientists is **defining for ourselves what we deem to be the ideal worker in this field**. How does one recognize an engineer or computer scientist as such? What is it about their work that is uniquely tied to their field? What kinds of traits, attributes, actions, or ways of being and knowing are valued? Although it is easy to recognize Latina students as the kind of people *capable* of engaging in this kind of work, the bigger question remains whether they should want to identify with these fields. It is imperative that equity-minded practitioners continue to question who they are asking Latina students to become during this process.

Concordia University Irvine

Engineering Degree, Irvine, California

Creating a new engineering program is never easy, particularly when we are trying to be thoughtful about who we are asking students to become and how we are defining for ourselves who the ideal worker in this field should be. Concordia University Irvine, a private Lutheran institution, distinguishes itself as a place in which students have the "freedom to explore [their] future and faith." The newly created bachelor of science in engineering degree promises to serve future engineers with broad training for the twenty-first century, interdisciplinary learning, and engagement in service to others and meeting the needs of communities. **Dr. Gabriela Espinosa, an assistant professor and founding director of the engineering program at Concordia University Irvine**, led the efforts to create these unique learning opportunities. Born in Nicaragua and raised in New York City, she attended Yale University for her bachelor's degree, St. Louis University for her master's in biomedical engineering, and then Washington University in St. Louis for her PhD in biomedical engineering. In founding the engineering degree program, Dr. Espinosa focused on creating an engineering experience that both spoke to her institution's unique context as an HSI and Christian-based liberal arts institution and the need to train a **"different type of engineer"** who has broad training, takes an interdisciplinary approach to learning and leading, and engages in service to others. She wanted to create an experience that had the potential not only to impact one's career but also to address the needs of society. Throughout the process, she and her team were dedicated to **distilling what it means to be an engineer**, which meant asking questions such as the following: What kind of engineer do we want as a graduate? How do we do human-centered design and serve our communities with our engineering skills? How do we build structures so students feel supported to live authentically and see engineers who look like them? Although Dr. Espinosa is committed to the success of all engineering students, she is particularly dedicated to ensuring that Latina students feel comfortable within their classrooms and labs, and she loves the culture that they have developed, in which Latina engineering students can be themselves. What I think is particularly compelling about this program and its work is that Dr. Espinosa is, as she describes, "unapologetically" herself and has committed to the creation of an engineering experience that encourages students (and those who serve them) to engage with their social and engineering identities in ways that benefit both the student at an individual level and society as a whole.

Reframing Who We Think of as Meaningful Identity Actors. Over time, Latina students in these fields have been socialized to believe that, other than one's own recognition, it is the recognition of peers, faculty, and industry partners that matters in the engineering and computing identity development process. However, I believe that it is only through **reframing who we think of as meaningful identity actors** that we can support Latina students on their identity journeys and break down tired tropes about whose perspective means something in engineering and computing.

Although **peer, faculty, and industry partner recognition** is essential in the identity process, there are others whose presence on this journey is often misunderstood or not fully realized. For example, although we know that families, staff members, and Latin* communities are important to the educational success of Latina students in these fields, we often marginalize their role in the identity process. **Family members**, both within these fields and outside them, play vital roles in supporting identity, encouraging Latina students to see themselves in these roles long before they may see their own potential, and sustaining their identities when the full weight and oppression of these fields threatens to swallow them up. Staff members who serve students day in and day out are often important actors in engineering and computing identity, particularly when students may feel disconnected from their peers or faculty members at the institution. **Latin* communities** often provide a sense of inspiration and paying it forward that sustains Latina students during difficult identity recognition clashes. Rather than marginalize individuals and groups who obviously have so much to offer our Latina students, it is our responsibility to leverage their influence by building relationships to better support students.

Your Trauma Is Not Her Trauma, So Stop It. So much of the discussion problematizing who we are asking Latina students to become is rooted in a distorted web of **intergenerational trauma**. Engineering and computing colleagues have experienced a range of trauma that influenced how they moved within the fields, including how they chose to form their own identities and interact with the next generation. *I went through it; so can you.* While a bit of academic struggle and shared experience can inspire a sense of community and camaraderie, truly traumatic identity recognition events, like those that I hear about from students across the country, are unnecessary and decimate students' sense of place within their fields.

Rather than building and sustaining identity, some practitioners within these fields see their role as that of a **gatekeeper who decides who is worthy** (and unworthy) of passing as an engineer or computer scientist. Individuals may adhere to a strict code of what it means to engage with the field, with little thought to how they have, whether directly or indirectly, forced a Latina student out or left her with so much trauma that she is forced to bury her own identities deep within her to identify with these fields. In contrast, equity-minded practitioners should move toward the belief that engineers and computer scientists can look, act, and move through the world in a range of ways. You should consider how you can create relationships that build up Latina students in historically and culturally affirming ways by making a commitment to end the perpetuation of trauma. In a practical sense, this could mean examining Latina experiences to identify where the most problematic identity moments are happening (e.g., the first year or middle years) and building relationships to address these issues and give Latina students a chance to perform and be recognized in their role as engineers and computer scientists. A commitment to ending the cycle of trauma represents a commitment to honoring the lives of Latina students and recognizing them as valued members of the engineering and computing communities capable of bringing a wealth of knowledge to those communities.

CONCLUSION

This chapter sought to address how we can build and sustain the relationships needed for developing engineering and computing identity. I covered how we can amplify interests through relationships that support Latina students as complex individuals and how we can expand competence and performance through relationship building that is dynamic and responsive to these students and their communities. I also explored what it might look like to intensify recognition opportunities by creating relationships that respect history, culture, and Latina ways of knowing. While support structures and relationship building are paramount to getting the work done, we must also engage in resistance to nurture engineering and computing identity if we are to truly transform the systems around us.

CHAPTER 7

Engaging in Resistance to Nurture Engineering and Computing Identity

Las nepantleras recognize that we're all complicit in the existing power structures, that we must deal with conflictive as well as connectionist relations within and among various groups. Ensuring that our acts not mirror or replicate the oppression and dominant power structures we seek to dismantle, las nepantleras upset our cultures' foundation and disturb the concepts structuring their realities.

–Gloria Anzaldúa[1]

The word *resistance* often refers to the ability of an individual or group to stand in opposition to a particular oppressive force. Acts of resistance can be both internal and external and manifest in the way we think, behave, or interact with others in our environment. Resistance conjures up different meanings and images for different people. While some find inspiration and comfort in the meanings of resistance, others see conflict and divisiveness. For some, the word stirs up images of more militant groups, like the Brown Berets,[2] whereas for others, it may invoke an image of a higher education practitioner quietly but fiercely navigating around oppressive policies and practices.

When I first conceived this book, it did not have a resistance chapter. However, with the proliferation of diversity, equity, and inclusion (DEI) bans across the country over time, it became apparent that it needed one. I could not, in good conscience, publish this book without addressing the need for resistance within our work. As of the writing of this book, countless bills have been signed into state law targeting DEI funding, practices, and promotion in colleges and universities.[3] Every day more bills are being introduced and are currently making their way through state legislative systems. Now more than ever, it is a moment to engage in resistance and be that equity-minded *nepantlera* in your work.

A Chicana feminist approach encourages us to do work that is transgressive, and as Gloria Anzaldúa states above, we are called to be *nepantleras* in the work that we do. *Nepantleras* are defined as "boundary-crossers, thresholders who initiate others in rites of passage, *activistas* who, from a listening, receptive, spiritual stance, rise to their own visions and shift into acting them out, hacienda *mundo* Nuevo (introducing change)."[4] *Nepantleras* live in the in between, often overcoming struggles, making sense of the world, building, inspiring others to action, and constantly moving between worlds, which is not without experiences of pain, isolation, and rejection.[5] Equity-minded practitioners could benefit from viewing the students they serve as well as themselves as *nepantleras*, navigating the borderlands of engineering and computing and committing to making identity formation as antioppressive and disruptive as possible.

Framing this work as resistance is important because it acknowledges that masculine and white supremacist norms and values exist and are often embedded in the engineering and computing work that we do. Even the work that we, or outsiders, might consider DEI can still be founded upon these norms and values. We must confront our own complicity and recognize how we position ourselves and our efforts to ensure that we are taking antioppressive approaches to support engineering and computing identity. This means challenging dominant power structures rather than replicating them and upsetting structures that have not served Latina students well. When thinking about engineering and computing identity, we must stay focused on what kind of individuals we are asking Latinas to become.

What are we *really* resisting against, and why? We must acknowledge the oppressive forces at play, such as racism, sexism, classism, and homophobia. We must recognize that there are very real, strategic, and coordinated forces that seek to systematically disassemble every vestige of DEI or Latina-specific work that we do. However, we cannot resort to mere handwringing. Latina students deserve equity-minded practitioners who will be the first ones to resist and act, rather than leave the battles to the students themselves. There is not a world in which we can engage in transformative action toward engineering and computing identity for Latina students without being clear about the oppressive forces that exist. It would be naïve to think that this kind of work could be done without needing to engage in acts of resistance.

Across our research studies, we have seen how powerful it is when Latina students engage in their own acts of resistance, not only articulating the wide range of problems that they see within their fields but also giving their time, energy, and spirit to resist marginalization. Students have refused to let faculty, peers, or higher education institutions define who they are as engineers or computer scientists. They have also called out racist, sexist, and classist structures and engaged in acts of internal (e.g., community transformation, healing) and external (e.g., engaging with an institution for reform) transformational resistance.[6] Whether through more individual-based forms of resistance, such as pushing toward success in order to inspire their Latina family members, or more public acts of resistance, such as participating in town halls or creating spaces exclusively for Latinas in engineering and computing, there is no doubt that Latinas *showed up*. Latina engineering and computing students are using their own resistant capital to challenge marginalization and actively reframe their experiences as trailblazing.[7] Many Latina students are in uncharted territory with the disciplines and careers that they have chosen, forging a trail both for their families and communities. As such, many students resist the existence of traditional metaphorical borders between Latin* communities and higher education spaces and instead seek to bridge the space between their institutions and their home communities and advocate for social justice.[8]

As such, I dedicate this chapter to all the Latina engineering and computing college students out there and hope that they know that their mere *existence* as well as their actions are beautiful forms of resistance. I also write this chapter as a guide for equity-minded practitioners, particularly those with marginalized identities who are resisting through their own presence, their actions, and their rest. I write for those equity-minded practitioners who see problems, critique them, and are moved to collective action, as well as those who seek to resist the essentialism or ephemeral nature of our present efforts. I write this as a love letter to all of you out there, deep in the trenches, engaging in resistance to nurture engineering and computing identity. This work that you do is valuable and worth your time, energy, and spirit.

A GAME PLAN FOR ENGAGING IN RESISTANCE

This chapter, outlined in figure 7.1, lays out a game plan for how equity-minded practitioners might pursue resistance efforts that nurture engineering and computing identity. The game plan includes four key strategies meant to support both equity-minded practitioners and the Latina students they serve. In this chapter, I explore my recommendations for how to:

- **Reconcile *la nepantlera* with the engineering and computing identity context by:**
    - Recognizing Latina students as boundary crossers
    - Acknowledging equity-minded practitioners as boundary crossers
    - Rejecting false dichotomies and complicating difference

FIGURE 7.1 Engaging in resistance to nurture engineering and computing identity

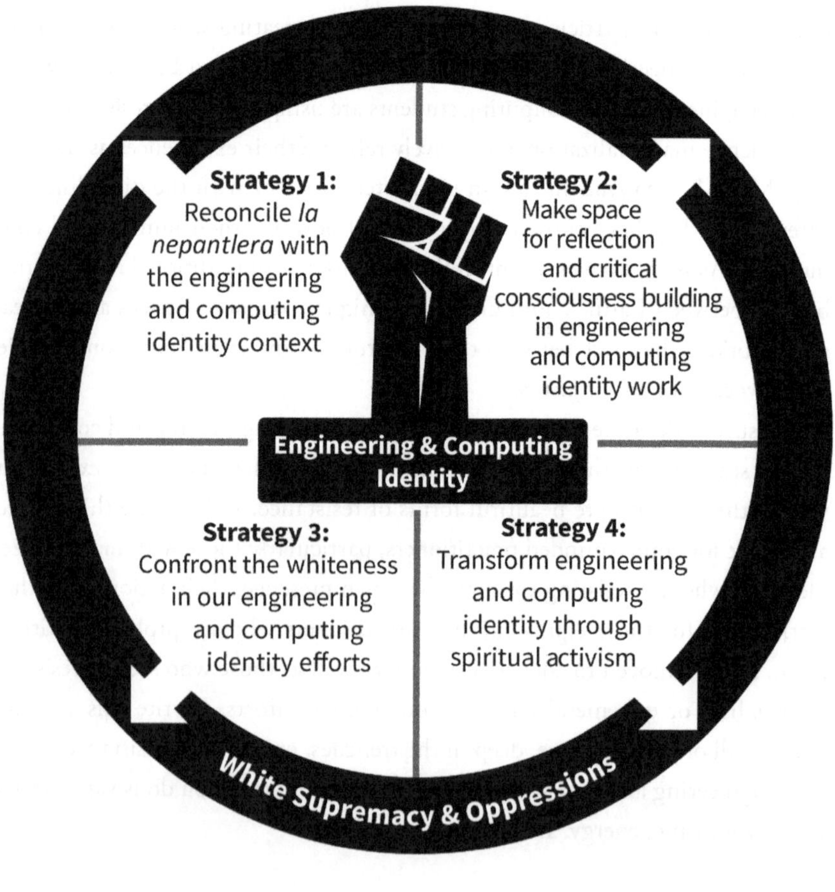

- **Make space for reflection and critical consciousness building in engineering and computing identity work by:**
    - Promoting reflective engagement
    - Dismantling persistent Latina stereotypes
    - Questioning who has power and why
- **Confront the whiteness in our engineering and computing identity efforts by:**
    - Knowing what whiteness looks like
    - Recognizing that we may be a part of the problem
    - Using our words and actions to name and address whiteness
- **Transform engineering and computing identity through spiritual activism by:**
    - Tying engineering and computing to spiritual activism
    - Doing the work of healing
    - Moving from "inner acts" to "public acts"
    - Engaging in self-care and self-love

STRATEGY 1: RECONCILING *LA NEPANTLERA* WITH THE ENGINEERING AND COMPUTING IDENTITY CONTEXT

The first strategy addresses how equity-minded practitioners must come to view both themselves and the students they work with as boundary crossers that move in between the borderlands of formal postsecondary education and community. This strategy calls on equity-minded practitioners to apply ideas of Anzaldúa's *la nepantlera* (discussed earlier in this chapter as well as in other sections of this book) as part of how they create student identity experiences and engage in resistance. An inherent part of this strategy is the need to reject false dichotomies and complicate difference to expand our understanding of the challenges and opportunities in this work. When we view the engineering and computing identity process as a boundary-crossing experience, we encourage not only ourselves but also those around us to resist the status quo and move toward change.

Latina Students as Boundary Crossers

Reconciling *la nepantlera* within engineering and computing identity contexts means viewing Latina students and the practitioners who work with them as boundary crossers. Every day, **Latina students cross physical, academic, emotional, social, and spiritual borders** where they must navigate the clashing of cultures. They are asked to exist in an in-between space in which the values and norms from their communities may come in stark contrast to those within engineering and computing. However, some practitioners may not acknowledge the work that Latina students are doing at the borderlands of their formal postsecondary education.

Latina students are often boundary crosses who, through their work with faculty members, academic support services, student organizations, and others, initiate change by creating rites of passage for their communities. That is, they are attempting to **create the *mundo nuevo*** that Anzaldúa alludes to—a new world in which Latin* communities can build and sustain their engineering and computing identities in a way that is authentic to them, rather than having them dictated by what institutions or employers see as the "right way." Recognizing Latina students as boundary crossers means acknowledging the lived experiences of students and the often-unnoticed labor that they do for themselves and those around them. Their ability to cross boundaries and embody their authentic engineering and computing identities is a form of resistance that should be encouraged and supported. It is with this knowledge that you can work toward eliminating barriers to access and success and creating opportunities for better engineering and computing identity experiences.

Society of Hispanic Professional Engineers

SHPEtinas, City of Industry, California, and Across the Country

When thinking of Latina students as *nepantleras* who are navigating the in-between spaces, my first thoughts are of the **Society of Hispanic Professional Engineers (SHPE)**, which has served as a consistent champion for Latin* students navigating these boundaries and, in effect, creating a new world in which more authentic engineering identities can thrive. Celebrating fifty years of service and advocacy, SHPE is the largest association in the United States for Latin* professionals in STEM (science, technology, engineering, and mathematics). Almost every Latina engineer who I have connected with, both in my research and professional networks, talks about the integral role that SHPE has played in her life. SHPE has had an indelible influence on the identity development of many Latina engineers, and I, myself, am a lifetime member because I believe in its mission and values to serve our community. SHPE offers a variety of culturally relevant programming, training, and mentorship aimed at empowering Latin* communities to realize their full potential and become valued and influential STEM contributors. SHPE values *familia* (a sense of family and collective strength), service, education, and resilience as an organization and offers a range of initiatives such as Noche de Ciencias (family science nights) and Equipando Padres, which seek to provide Latin* students and families with resources, as well as Familia Stories, which feature stories about SHPE members on platforms such as the SHPE OutLoud Podcast, newsletters, and Instagram. SHPE also conducts research on its members that has provided insight into the experiences of Latin* students in engineering (and STEM) from across the nation's membership.

However, perhaps my favorite aspect of SHPE is the organization's commitment to their Latina members through SHPEtinas. **Yamille Pérez, SHPEtinas Conference Chair of the SHPE National Convention Planning Committee**, works with a team of volunteer undergraduate students and professionals nationwide to execute a series of Latina-focused events, including workshops, panels, and meals, for more than four hundred attendees. **SHPEtinas** is all about Latina women working and succeeding together and creating a space that empowers women with confidence and collective strength. It provides a space in which Latinas can be in community with each other to network and build capacity. In particular, through the SHPEtinas conference, Latinas from across the nation come together to immerse themselves in sessions that support technical and leadership development as well as promote candid, meaningful conversations about Latina experiences.

Across the nation, and especially at institutions like **Virginia Tech and Texas A&M University College Station**, SHPE chapters have created their own SHPEtinas groups that aim to engage Latina engineers (and other STEM students) in activities that address the importance of Latina representation and address discrimination head on while creating close bonds among Latinas. What I love about SHPEtinas is that it, without ever directly stating this, attends to engineering identity development in a way that exhibits many of the hallmarks of a Chicana feminist approach. SHPEtinas attends to issues of engineering identity recognition—one of the most important elements of identity for Latina students—and provides opportunities for building interests, knowledge, and skills while attending to gender identity issues that remain present in our community. The space the SHPEtinas has created, both at the national and chapter levels, is asset based and collective in nature and moves Latina members toward resisting the white, masculine norms that pervade engineering and other STEM fields.

Equity-Minded Practitioners as Boundary Crossers

For many of you, and particularly those of you with marginalized identities, the concept of educational borderlands and being in a **constant state of boundary crossing** may be all too familiar. You are the ones on your campus initiating rites of passage for students, encouraging activism, and quietly, or loudly, pushing for change and trying to break down structural inequities. You are the ones helping to coordinate SHPE or Latin* graduation events. You are the ones pushing for more culturally relevant curriculum. **You are the ones supporting Latina students** as they navigate a difficult transition to an engineering or computing context. You live it. First, I would like to applaud you for your efforts. So often, it is individuals like you who do not get the proper credit for doing the work that you do, day in and day out. You may cross those same physical, academic, emotional, social, and spiritual borders that Latina students are crossing every day. Recognize the fortitude and resiliency that you, as a border crosser, have had in the past and continue to have each day. And do not let that status go unnoticed. Latina students need to hear from you about your experience navigating these borderlands and know that, should they need it, you can act as a navigator for them as they cross back and forth between the borderlands.

For others, particularly those equity-minded practitioners from majority backgrounds or who are early in their careers, the idea of boundary crossing and initiating change toward a new understanding of identity may be a newer concept. Although committed to equity work, you might not have thought about how you, yourself, cross these boundaries in your own way. Or perhaps you truly *do not* cross any borders because the culture and structures of engineering and computing within higher education were made for you. In that case, ask why and how that privilege happened and how you can use this knowledge for improving opportunities for Latina students. In either case, viewing yourself as a boundary crosser is powerful for understanding and dismantling persistent gatekeeping that inhibits Latina students from viewing themselves in engineering and computing roles.

Rejecting False Dichotomies and Complicating Differences

Engaging in engineering and computing identity work that resists white supremacist norms and values means rejecting the many false dichotomies that limit our thinking and complicating difference within the many aspects of the work. **False dichotomies would have us believe in limited, simple choices**, rather than the expansive and often complicated nature of the identity experience. For example, Latina students should not have to choose whether they are part of the women's group or the Latin* community; Latina students should not have to choose between their Black, queer, or other identities and their engineering and computing identities. Likewise, resistance efforts cannot be centered in one space or merely attend to the racial or ethnic identities of Latina students but must **attend to the present intersectional boundary-crossing experiences** that these students undergo to build and maintain their identities. As *nepantleras*, it is the responsibility of practitioners to move beyond this either/or thinking or essentializing of the experiences of Latina students and recognize that resistance efforts become stronger as we work together toward more inclusive, expansive views of the engineering and computing identity experience.

STRATEGY 2: MAKING SPACE FOR REFLECTION AND CRITICAL CONSCIOUSNESS BUILDING IN ENGINEERING AND COMPUTING IDENTITY WORK

The second strategy addresses how equity-minded practitioners integrate reflection and critical consciousness building into engineering and computing identity work. One of the most salient concepts within Chicana feminism is the need to continuously dig deeper within our own experiences and awaken to what is both within and around us.[9] In the context of engineering and computing identity, reflection and critical consciousness building refer to how students and practitioners pursue a path toward an understanding of themselves as well as knowledge of identity-related issues (and the sociohistorical contexts that created them) and engage in forms of resistance against larger systems of oppression. It is from this heightened critical consciousness that students and practitioners can work toward dismantling persistent Latina stereotypes and questioning who has power and why.

Reflective Engagement

Reflective engagement asks us to consider how we understand our world and our interactions with others in the world. Doing reflective engagement with an eye toward resistance means interrogating why we have chosen this equity-minded practitioner path as well as what changes we might want to see and why. **Coming to consciousness**, whether about one's own engineering and computing identity or one's support of Latina students on this journey, requires extensive reflective engagement.

An awareness of one's own mind might look like confronting one's ways of doing and knowing, including a greater understanding of one's place and purpose in the world. On a personal level, **stepping into critical consciousness** might mean exploring your own positionality, including who you are to the work and how you got to where you are. For example, in workshops I do, I like to have audience members engage in a short activity in which they look at three sets of questions: self-study, individual level of change, and institutional level of change:

1. **The self-study:** What elements of engineering/computing identity development were critical to your own journey and identity?
    a. How did you get interested?
    b. What kinds of knowledge and skills did you learn? How did you *know* that you knew them?
    c. What did "acting like" an engineering or computer scientist *look* like?
    d. Who were the important people who recognized you (or did not recognize you) as an engineer or computer scientist?
2. **The individual level of change:** How can I encourage engineering/computing identity development for students?
    a. How can I get more Latina students interested in engineering/computing?
    b. What *knowledge and skills* do I think they need to know? How do I impart those?

c. What *experiences, actions, or behaviors* do they need to have? How do I integrate these?
d. Who, outside of the students themselves, needs to *see Latina students* as engineers or computer scientists?
e. How do my efforts act as a form of resistance against white, masculine norms?

3. **The institutional level of change:** How can my institution encourage engineering/computing identity development for Latina students?
    a. How can we leverage resources to increase interest, competence, and performance?
    b. How do we scale and assess these kinds of changes?
    c. How do we attend to intersectional identities and systemic oppressions?
    d. How do institutional efforts act as a form of resistance against white, masculine norms?

An exercise like this one can help you step into critical consciousness, first by thinking about your own experience, then moving out to the individual level and eventually the institutional level of change. Inherent in an activity like this one is the recognition that engineering and computing identity occurs within highly contextualized spaces and that our efforts toward better, identity-forward strategies must be meaningful and strategic.

This can be **a kind of awakening** in which you might see yourself and your work as a site of resistance. An awakening to the experiences of *individuals* in your life might mean "seeing" Latina students, circumstances, and actions and considering the underlying needs and desires of these students, while an awakening to the *world* around you might mean understanding those elements of the Latina student experience within the sociohistorical context in which they happened. Consciousness building encourages practitioners, regardless of their identities or backgrounds, to step into knowing and understanding and to serve students more fully in asset-based, multidimensional ways.

In a rapidly changing world like ours, it is **the opportunity to reflect that sets us apart and strengthens our own spirit** and our efforts. To promote reflective engagement, practitioners can integrate opportunities for reflecting into the strategic planning process or when shaping programming meant to enhance engineering and computing identity formation. They can also ask colleagues to explore their own positionalities, privileges, biases, and journeys to more fully understand how they are coming to the work and how they engage (or thwart in some cases) resistance efforts of the group. These reflections can help practitioners to better understand themselves and their resistance efforts and can reveal to leaders how to better serve their colleagues and engage in collective resistance efforts.

We must **set aside time within curricula or otherwise to do the deep dive** needed to be truly reflective about the identity experiences of Latina students and map out resistance efforts. Although creating time and space to reflect is critical for practitioners, it is also critical that we create this space for Latina students in engineering and computing. You should encourage Latina students to self-reflect and push toward a deeper understanding of their engineering or computing journeys, including their decision-making processes and how they are making sense of their programs. It is important that this reflection be highly tailored to the task and taken seriously by all involved. Through reflective engagement, equity-minded practitioners can help Latina students explore their and others' worldviews, which will help them to better understand themselves as well as different viewpoints, a skill that may be particularly helpful in working with engineering and computing teams throughout the educational and workforce journeys.

Dismantling Persistent Latina Stereotypes

Part of reflection and coming to consciousness involves **liberating Latina students from persistent stereotypes** and interrogating how we as practitioners and the structures around us (some of our own making) uphold systems of power and privilege. Dismantling persistent Latina stereotypes requires us to know what the stereotypes are, where they came from, and how they are harmful to students' identity. Latina students experience both gendered and racialized stereotypes (as well as a host of others).

Worn out stereotypes we must combat include tropes about the young Latina mother, the docile (or angry) Latina, and the oversexualized, feisty Latina. These stereotypes, which come from myriad sources both outside of and inside the Latin* community, are the result of patriarchal and white supremacist structures in our society meant to control and limit the narratives and lives of Latina women. As Latina students build their engineering and computing identities, these stereotypes cause harm by influencing how peers and institutional partners view and interact with them. Whether overtly or through unconscious biases, these stereotypes persist.

The National Center for Women and Information Technology

TECHNOLOchicas, Boulder, Colorado

TECHNOLOchicas is an initiative of the National Center for Women and Information Technology (NCWIT) focused on dismantling stereotypes and supporting Latina women in computing by building relationships among Latina students, families, educators, and industry partners. **Yvonne De La Pena, Lead Consultant for the TECHNOLOchicas initiative,** collaborates with NCWIT leadership to plan and execute the TECHNOLOchicas initiative. This initiative presents stereotype-shattering stories of Latina technologists through television, social media, online videos, and events to inspire young women to pursue careers and persist in STEM. The TECHNOLOchicas initiative is made up of two main parts: Technolochicas Stars and Technolochicas Code It. **Technolochicas Stars** is an awareness-raising campaign that highlights the stories of Latinas in computing through the sharing of Latina stories and activation of Latina ambassadors across the nation. The stories shared highlight the different kinds of careers that Latinas in computing have, while the ambassadors volunteer at workshops, organize outreach, and are a resource to inspire Latina youth. **Technolochicas Code It** focuses on providing courses that familiarize Latina students with computing concepts and training mentors to support this computing success. The program partners with schools and universities to train mentors in courses related to website development, app and game development, artificial intelligence, and robotics. Those mentors then train Latina students on the content and support students in completing computing projects and engaging with the TECHNOLOchicas community.

What I love about NCWIT's support of TECHNOLOchicas is the acknowledgement of the important contribution that Latinas have made to the world of computing. This signals the honoring of Latina ways of knowing and an investment in Latina students and professionals in ways that affirm their gender and racial/ethnic identities. TECHNOLOchicas, through its sharing of stories and activation of the Latina computing community, is also an example of resistance against persistent stereotypes and the dominant narrative and demonstrates that Latina students and professionals are successfully engaging and thriving in computing in ways that are authentic to them.

To dismantle biases and stereotypes, we must first **educate ourselves about who Latina students are and what unconscious (or conscious) biases** we have. This includes unconscious bias training or engaging in reflective exercises, particularly ones that force us to look inward at ourselves and our actions. Once we understand our own biases, it is also our responsibility to dismantle those stereotypes by connecting with Latina students and their communities to create a new, asset-based narrative of who these students and communities really are, beyond the limiting stereotypes.

Questioning Who Has Power and Why

Another part of coming to critical consciousness and engaging in resistance efforts is building a clear **understanding of the landscape around you**. However, we only get a partial view of that landscape—the sociohistorical context, the present numbers, and the existing programming—if we fail to pay attention to **who has power and why**. While consciousness must begin with an inward look, engagement in true resistance identity work is a disruption and rebalancing of power. This disruption allows Latina students to exist in engineering and computing spaces more authentically and to build their professional identities.

To explore the current power structures, practitioners should consider **who gets to sit at the decision-making table and whose voices are most often heard**. Who gets to decide what an engineering or computing person should look like or behave like? Who are the individuals or groups that get to define how money is spent or how priorities are set? Answering these questions will illuminate who has power and how that power is wielded on a daily, yearly, and long-term basis. From there, practitioners can interrogate why these decisions were made and what forces are present (e.g., institutionally, legislatively) that have placed power where it is and perpetuated action or inaction. It is from these understandings that practitioners can begin to tailor their resistance efforts toward a redistribution of power and a more Chicana feminist–informed approach to identity. Similar questions might be posed to Latina students about their engineering and computing experiences, or students can be given exercises to encourage them to explore what they know about the type of people who go into engineering and computing fields and the existing hierarchies within college settings.

STRATEGY 3: CONFRONTING THE WHITENESS IN OUR ENGINEERING AND COMPUTING IDENTITY EFFORTS

The third strategy addresses how equity-minded practitioners can confront the whiteness in our engineering and computing identity efforts. This includes knowing what whiteness looks like, recognizing how practitioners contribute to the problem, and using words and actions to name and address it. If there was ever a topic in engineering and computing identity efforts that scared and polarized practitioners, it would be that of whiteness. The discussion of whiteness within higher education spaces and, more specifically, in engineering and computing spaces is growing.[10] Whiteness is ubiquitous within the engineering and computing fields, and yet it is the elephant in the room—the thing we generally do not want to confront, do not want to understand, and do not want to target. However, when practitioners talk about "broadening participation" or use any of those other seemingly neutral terms and phrases, what we *really* should be talking about is a systematic confrontation with the whiteness in our engineering and computing communities. We did not stumble into these frightening statistics and hostile learning environments by chance; they were the fruit borne out of many years of systemic racism and the oppression of Latin* communities, not just in the United States, but across the world.

Scholars have outlined—far more deftly and eloquently than me—the persistence and danger of whiteness to the educational experiences and workforce trajectories of our students and laid out answers as to how to root out and resist whiteness.[11] We should *all* be reading and invoking their work as we think about how to take an antioppressive approach to engineering and computing identity for Latina students. And although there are many approaches to how we might confront whiteness in our higher education contexts, there are a few that I believe to be especially salient in the discussion of Latina identity in these fields. Practitioners should know what whiteness looks like, be willing to recognize themselves as part of the problem, and use their words and actions to name and address it.

Knowing What Whiteness Looks Like

To understand whiteness and how it influences engineering and computing identity, practitioners should **understand white privilege, white supremacy, and white fragility.**[12] White privilege refers to the benefits that white people receive through their membership of a dominant group. There are certain privileges white people experience—so clearly laid out in texts like Peggy McIntosh's *White Privilege: Unpacking the Invisible Knapsack*—like seeing themselves represented on college campuses or within engineering and computing fields, which Latina students do not experience.[13] We are in a world in which elements of white supremacy continue to exist, both those that are overt in nature (e.g., discrimination, murder), which almost everyone can agree are wrong, and those that are more covert (e.g., color-evasiveness, denial of racism, colorism), which can be less apparent to us. Part of knowing what whiteness means is understanding that whiteness comes in many forms and exists in a variety of settings, creating an entire ecosystem that Latina students must navigate to build and sustain engineering and computing identities and persist within their fields.

All of us—Latin* individuals and communities, included—can perpetuate whiteness and upholding of white supremacy. Some practitioners do this by pushing assimilationist ideology on Latina students, asking them to shrink themselves to make others feel comfortable or conform to our ideal version of what an engineer or computer scientist should look and act like. Similarly, other practitioners may inadvertently perpetuate whiteness and white supremacy when they use color-evasive language, purporting to "not see color," or expect Latina students to modify aspects of their identity, personal appearance, or interactions with their community to come more in line with what society expects from engineering and computing students. If you are looking for a good resource of what whiteness looks like, read the article "White Supremacy Culture – Still Here" by Tema Okun, which provides examples as well as antidotes to the problems posed by whiteness.[14]

Recognizing We May Be Part of the Problem

Few equity-oriented practitioners I know would readily admit that they are perpetuating whiteness in their thinking or actions. **None of us want to believe that *we* are the problem.** It is easier to believe that the problem lies outside of us, rather than within us or in our actions. However, if we take a moment to consider the possibility that we are part of the problem, in so many cases, we will realize that—with the best of intentions—we have replicated marginalizing structures. We may have, unwittingly, created policies, practices, and programming that are steeped in white privilege and uphold white supremacy and fragility, even though it looks like typical (or even award-winning) DEI work. Equity-minded practitioners should interrogate why certain policies exist as well as who truly benefits from certain practices and programming and whether there are opportunities to make these initiatives more liberatory and less white centric.

Using Your Words and Actions to Name and Address Whiteness

Knowing and understanding whiteness and inequities is pointless without the **ability to use your words and actions to call it out**. I will provide an example here. For years, I felt wildly uncomfortable with what whiteness was and how I was complicit in perpetuating it. I even felt resistant to saying the words *racism* and *whiteness* out loud or using them in my writing. I thought it might be too much for me to actually identify what I saw as racism. Maybe what I was seeing did not elevate to the level of racism or perhaps what people were doing was not really whiteness? Now, looking back, I realize that the Latina student experiences I was writing about were incredibly racist (among other forms of oppression); I just did not see it. It was not until one of my dear friends, Dr. Beth Bukoski, after reading my work, challenged me to say the words—to name them clearly and without abandonment. The irony of a white woman having to say this *to me*, a Latina, for me to fully get it is not lost on me. However, that day, her expertise as an intersectional gender scholar and social justice advocate had a profound effect on my life as a scholar.

My life has forever been changed since that moment, and I have tried (and failed sometimes) to ensure that I am naming and acting in resistance to whiteness in ways that are authentic to me. Likewise, equity-minded practitioners must be empowered to name and act against whiteness within their spheres of influence. I am calling for both personal introspection and systematic change. On a personal level, we cannot allow ourselves to be shackled to white supremacy and sit within the comforts of white fragility to protect ourselves and our feelings of comfort.[15] We must examine our own personal experiences and interactions that may be steeped in whiteness.

At a systematic level, this means **examining current engineering and computing identity practices for elements of whiteness**, voicing those concerns, and shifting approaches to address whiteness. Put plainly, if any of these efforts are steeped in traditionally white norms and values or inhibit Latina students from having a strong engineering or computing identity, you should consider removing them. For example, white supremacy values individualism and competition, while many Latina students, in general, prefer to work and interact more collaboratively. If classrooms and programs are created with individualism and competition as foundational values, then Latina students may have difficulty seeing themselves in the role of an engineer or computer scientist. In this case, equity-minded practitioners might consider other ways of structuring the learning environment that are more inclusive and collaborative. And although dismantling whiteness within identity formation experiences may take time, particularly if those activities or policies are successful in today's landscape, practitioners should continue to resist against whiteness to make way for approaches that enable Latina engineering and computing students to have even greater identity-affirming experiences.

STRATEGY 4: TRANSFORMING ENGINEERING AND COMPUTING IDENTITY THROUGH SPIRITUAL ACTIVISM

The fourth strategy addresses how practitioners can transform engineering and computing identity through spiritual activism. Although engineering and computing are not traditionally thought of as sites of spiritual activism, I challenge practitioners to consider them in this way. Spiritual activism is a worldview, created by Gloria Anzaldúa, that emphasizes the importance of spirituality to the work that we do and highlights the interconnectedness of the world as well as one's mind, body, and spirit.[16] Drawing from these ideas, equity-minded practitioners can view engineering and computing identity work as a spiritual, healing act, both individually and collectively, that requires self-care.

Tying Engineering and Computing to Spiritual Activism

To do this work, we must explicitly acknowledge the role of spiritual activism. It is a call to action for social transformation and change. Engineering and computing identity work is **not just an intellectual exercise but, for many, a spiritual journey** on which mind, body, and soul are doing the work. Identity work can be simultaneously powerful and transformative because it constantly asks us who our students (or in some cases we ourselves) are becoming. Its power rests in its ability to shape students' interests, competence and performance, and ability to feel recognized as the kind of person who does engineering or computing. It is transformative because it has the capability to alter people's career trajectories, financial standing, and value systems in addition to the way students think about their place within engineering and computing settings as well as the broader world.

Although engineering and computing identity is often a continuous journey for *nepantleras*, Anzaldúa reminds us that living in that in-between and "unstable, unpredictable, precarious" world is not without pain.[17] As an answer to that pain and struggle, Chicana feminists recognize the importance of **spiritual activism to connect one's whole being with the work**. Spiritual activism emphasizes interconnectedness "with the world, with one's ancestors and descendants, and contemporary relations. . . . [It] connects the mind, the body, and the spirit, and in doing so, is a significant tool for the introspective work."[18] In addition, it is only by releasing "our resistance to embracing the spiritual realm . . . [that there can be an] energetic shift, hate can be transformed to love, competition to cooperation."[19]

However, without **honoring the spirituality and mind-body-spirit connection** inherent within engineering and computing identity work, this work is at risk of feeling hollow or betraying its true power. While traditional Western ideologies might ask us to create distance between spirituality and educational spaces, Chicana feminism reminds us that it is through spiritual activism that we can come to understand the interconnectedness of the issues facing Latina students in engineering and computing and more fully allow ourselves to become a part of the work that we do. For students, honoring engineering and computing identity development as a spiritual act might look like acknowledging the role of spirituality and ways of knowing beyond the merely intellectual or scientific, particularly during activities that may have traditionally been thought of as purely technical (e.g., design, coding). For practitioners, this might mean recognizing or rewarding identity development efforts that emphasize the mind-body-spirit connection or make interdisciplinary connections with individuals or groups who value spiritual activism as a form of resistance.

Doing the Work of Healing

The ability of spiritual activism to do the work of healing previous wounds is particularly important for Latina students in computing and engineering, as well as for the equity-minded practitioners who serve them. Within these fields, **Latina students may have experienced deep wounds of oppression** perpetuated by faculty, peers, and community members who did not value their presence or perspective. In this way, spiritual activism and the act of healing serve as forms of resistance by strengthening the Latina community and righting injustices that they have had to face in engineering and computing spaces. A Chicana feminist approach to healing asks us to uphold the connections between mind, body, and soul when engaging in resistance against oppression. The mind enables you to be aware of the world, to think and feel, whereas the body, your flesh and bones, allows you to move and engage with the physical world. Your soul is that almost indescribable essence of what makes you *you*. As equity-minded practitioners, all three of these elements must work in tandem to do this work.

Dora

Engineering Identity as a Means of Healing and Resistance

For some Latina students, getting to the college engineering experience is a culmination of a series of personal and educational traumas for which they are searching for healing. Engineering identity development can be a means of healing and an act of resistance for students in their educational journeys. Dora was a Latina immigrant who arrived from Central America to the United States when she was a small child. During her childhood, she experienced a series of traumas that left her distrustful and weary of men as well as depressed and anxious. Growing up in a world of trauma, poverty, crime, and limited career opportunities, she wanted something better for herself and her future. She was tired of other people dictating how her life would be. She wanted the power to decide what her life would look like and how she would heal from these traumas and move through the world. She saw it as her life's work to become a successful engineer in a "man's world," so she used her engineering education as a form of resistance. Despite being uncomfortable surrounded by men, she pursued an engineering degree.

Year after year, she encountered men, both white and Latino, who would try to sideline her from engineering projects and compete with her for who was right, who was wrong, and who got more recognition from peers, faculty, and employers. As such, she often felt the need to prove herself—to prove that she belonged in engineering and that she was just as competent as her male peers—and was often forced to work independently to gain access to opportunities. She watched other Latinas at her research-intensive predominately white institution leave the engineering program each year, but she loved engineering and endured. She loved launching rockets, doing outreach, and seeing her designs come to life. She refused to be marginalized and just kept coming back to her interests, her desire to see herself as an engineer, and the need for her to prevent others from being marginalized within the engineering environment. To heal from her experiences, she saw it as part of her purpose to inspire and support Latina students, among others, in their pursuit of an engineering degree. In particular, she loved sharing her love of engineering with young girls and watching them be inspired to do the work. Thus, Dora became an active participant in K–12 outreach activities such as engineering camps and elementary school visits, hoping that she could be a good role model for Latinas who come after her. In doing this, she began doing the work of healing from the trauma that she had experienced.

To begin the healing process, it can be helpful to commit to a **Body-Soul Rooted Pedagogy.**[20] A Body-Soul Rooted Pedagogy emphasizes education as a political act and site of resistance and empowerment that centers Latina ways of knowing and a sense of connectedness. This teaching approach takes a critical approach to navigating oppression, using teaching as a social action that can inspire hope, well-being, creativity, and connectedness to heal students. Built on the work of Chicana feminists,[21] this approach emphasizes creativity and connectedness as spiritual healing and can be used throughout the engineering and computing experience, particularly around reflection activities that ask students to place themselves in the work that they are doing.

Furthermore, equity-minded practitioners might consider ways to encourage Latina students to **trust their own cultural intuition**. Trusting one's cultural intuition means valuing Latina ways of knowing and concentrating on an individual's existing knowledge and experiences as well as reflecting on the individual and collective experience.[22] In engineering and computing, this might mean creating opportunities for Latina students to build on their own experiences and honor their existing forms of engineering and computing knowledge and skills. In addition, practitioners might also consider making space for Latina students to reflect on their own engineering and computing experiences (e.g., undergraduate research, lab work, classes) both individually and collectively to make sense of these experiences. This could be particularly helpful in scaffolding experiential learning opportunities and problem-solving activities.

To encourage Latina students to trust their own cultural intuition and heal, it can also be helpful for practitioners to open up opportunities for **pursuing truth telling and empowerment**. Pursuing truth telling emphasizes the importance of Latina students telling their own truth and choosing to acknowledge, rather than ignore, the significance of oppression and pain that individuals and groups have experienced throughout the education system, with the ultimate goal of empowerment and liberation. Here, truth is seen as a means to bring injustices and inequities to light. As Teresa Córdova writes, "The writings of Chicanas and women of color remind us that not only is the personal political, but when experiences are expressed so deeply, the personal is profound."[23] Giving Latina students an opportunity to express their perspectives and be truly heard may reveal not only more about the individual experience but also about the collective experiences of these students within your institution, opening up ways to face (possibly difficult) truths.

Another approach to healing is by **leveraging the concepts of community cultural wealth (CCW) and funds of identity (FOI) for engineering and computing identity development**. At an individual level, this approach can act as a transformative mechanism of healing from the barrage of challenges that students may face. On a broader level, CCW and FOI have the potential to honor Latin* ways of knowing and honor the communities that have been wounded over time and for generations. For example, practitioners can assist students with understanding their own CCW as well as FOI, including having students think about their home communities and the lessons, or *consejos*, that they have accumulated. This might involve taking time to dive into the literature and current practices around supporting CCW and FOI, including connecting with experts in this area to integrate an asset-based approach most effectively into the work that individuals and groups already do. Advising and support staff might also seek to spotlight students who have successfully used their CCW and FOI to shape their careers. These spotlights could be in the form of expert student panels in which multiple students share how they have leveraged their CCW and FOI for success or creating videos or other content around campus (e.g., posters, screens) that do so. Practitioners could also embed this into assignments, including asking Latina students to share what life experiences contributed to elements such as idea generation and design to get students thinking explicitly about their background and prior experiences.

You might also consider **exploring your own CCW and FOI** by unpacking what elements from your own home communities, families, and backgrounds have shaped your identities and careers. You might invite a facilitator to guide your group through the assets that each person brings to the higher education setting and encourage students to think about how they are bringing diverse forms of cultural wealth and funds of knowledge and identity into their educational experiences. You might then also consider how you can encourage identity development by providing navigational capital to Latina students (e.g., changing majors, responding to cultural clashes), inspiring aspirational capital (e.g., resilience in the face of challenges, maintaining hope), and drawing upon values of Latin* cultures to keep Latina students engaged with their field of study (e.g., giving back to the Latin* community, *familismo*, work ethic).

DIY Girls

Invent Girls and Girls Action Network and Support (GANAS), San Fernando, California

If you are looking for an organization that is truly doing the work of healing and strengthening our Latina community, DIY Girls is it. The real testament for this organization is their commitment for doing community- and place-based work in the San Fernando Valley, in which Latin* communities have a long history. DIY Girls is an organization focused on empowering girls and gender-expansive youth to explore STEAM (STEM plus arts) through programming that builds skills, confidence, and community. DIY

Girls uses an identity-forward approach to career exploration for Latina students, who make up most of its participants. **Susana Gomez, director of external affairs and communications**, described to me how the organization uses social and emotional learning, as well as justice, diversity, equity, and inclusion, to frame their work and draw from a talented group of mostly Latina practitioners and alumni to serve Latina students from elementary school through their transition to college. While all programs in DIY Girls are identity forward, I would like to highlight a few elements that are particularly of interest to the readers of this book.

Invent Girls, a year-long program focused on connecting high-school-aged girls to engineering skills and processes, engages Latina students in an Arduino-based project that builds on their exposure to teamwork, coding, three-dimensional design and printing, hardware assembly, programming, and soldering. They start the year with a series of mini-projects leading up to a final capstone project and wrap up their experience with a showcase for family members where they present their final project. Another program, their alumni network, is called **GANAS (Girls Action Network and Support)**, which in Spanish roughly translates to desire, want, or an urge to do something. This program keeps college graduates plugged into and identifying as "DIY Girls" long after their formal participation has ended. DIY Girls engages the alumni community with mixers and industry partner events and leverages their expertise for programming with younger Latina students. GANAS allows for an exchange of ideas and experiences between current DIY Girls and DIY Girl alums, allowing the *testimonios* of Latina students to be shared and for important *consejos* and CCW to be transmitted. Once a DIY Girl, always a DIY Girl. Although there are many reasons to absolutely love DIY Girls and the work that they do, for me, it is the commitment to serving Latina students and their communities that truly shines through and empowers these students to craft engineering and computing identities that are culturally rooted and allow them to be their authentic selves. In the San Fernando Valley, DIY Girls is a testament to the kind of healing work that can result from an intergenerational, connected, and culturally relevant approach to serving Latina girls and women.

Moving from "Inner Acts" to "Public Acts"

Engaging in resistance means gradually moving from **"inner acts" (which focus on the self) to "public acts" (which focus on changing the world around you).**[24] The inner acts of engineering and computing identity often look like a recursive series of defining and redefining what it means to be an engineer or computer scientist based on one's own competence and performance, interest, and recognition. It can be a highly introspective process by which Latina students make sense of their daily experiences with themselves and others within the context of their educational experiences. **Inner acts can lead to an awakening or reawakening of the self** and provide much needed centering to be able to do the heavy lifting of identity throughout their college careers. Referenced in earlier chapters, inner acts of resistance could look like Latina students taking control of their educational pathways by designing an educational plan that forefronts their engineering and computing interests or enhancing their help-seeking behaviors to support competence and performance building. However, a Chicana feminist approach might suggest that it is the move to "public acts" that can transform identity work from something that is beneficial to one Latina student, or just a few, to something that is more powerful, reaching other Latinas as well as Latin* communities. In previous chapters, some public acts of resistance that were discussed included Latina students forming identity-based computing organizations, engaging in outreach activities, or participating in design activities that engage Latina students with their local communities.

Kiara

Computing Identity as Resistance and Paving the Way for the Next Generation

Sometimes public acts are slow to roll out. However, a Latina student's computing identity journey can be a form of resistance and pave the way for the next generation of Latina computer scientists. Kiara, a computing major at a Hispanic-serving university, had some prior knowledge of coding before starting college, but upon entering college, it felt like everyone had so much more experience than she did. She constantly compared herself to others, noting their coding backgrounds and the vast experiences with computing that she just had not been exposed to yet. She felt a sense of imposter syndrome—like peers, faculty, and employers would soon realize that she, indeed, did not belong in her program. However, a transformative shift happened, and over time, she connected with teaching assistants, computing faculty, and student organizations that helped her refine her interests, knowledge, and skills, and ultimately nurtured her computing identity. Her sense of belonging and computing identity became further solidified after her first corporate internship, and after being mentored by several people with minoritized identities, she knew that this was the role for her. She began to transform into a Latina woman who was confident in her abilities to problem solve, learn challenging computing concepts, and be recognized by her computing community. As she progressed through her computing degree, she started to notice just how underrepresented Latina students were in computing, despite the institution's location in a city with a large Latin* population. She decided that she wanted to "pave the way for the next generation" and change a field that did not typically look like her. Although she grew into her computing identity, Kiara does not want other Latina students to feel the pains of imposter syndrome or feel unsupported at any time. She feels as though it is her duty to the Latina students who come after her to share her knowledge, give back, and resist the dominant narrative about who can be in computing.

Equity-minded practitioners can **move Latina students toward more public acts** by encouraging them to share their identity experiences with the campus as well as providing opportunities for students to become publicly engaged engineers or computer scientists that actively make connections to the communities around them. This move from inner acts to public ones is also an opportunity to connect Latina students to relationships that will guide them through the identity process as well as inspire them to become active in pursuing resistance and equity. However, care should be taken with these opportunities so as not to overly burden students with requests to share their experiences with others. Placing additional burdens on Latina students could negatively affect their engineering and computing identity and stifle their desire for resistance. However, as we move toward legislative environments that are increasingly anti-DEI, inspiring Latina students toward more public acts may be a means by which equity-minded practitioners can encourage work to continue as led by students.

Engaging in Self-Care and Self-Love

While I believe the work described in this chapter is meaningful, I also acknowledge that **equity-minded practitioners must take care of themselves** if they are to contribute to the movement toward better identity practices for Latina students in engineering and computing. Self-care is a conscious action of taking steps to preserve yourself and your physical and mental well-being; self-love is caring about yourself enough to continue caring about yourself at every step in your practitioner journey. Engaging in self-care and love honors the legacy of Chicana feminists such as Gloria Anzaldúa, who departed this world all too soon.

As practitioners committed to this work, you must be committed to the long and often difficult road that is educational change. We must invest in our own well-being because, as Chicana feminism reminds us, **no one will be there to save us—we must save ourselves**. Equity-minded practitioners who hold multiple marginalized identities (e.g., women, queer folx, people of color) must especially take care of themselves if they are to continue doing meaningful, transformative work.

Although self-care these days is increasingly tied to capitalist definitions of what it means to honor your mind, body, and spirit (e.g., luxury spa days, beauty products), the Latina students in engineering and computing who we serve deserve more than that from us. The kind of care that you need is that which truly speaks to **what restores you and helps you to be your best self** so that you can support Latina students in engineering and computing. This can mean taking time off, meditating, sleeping, learning to say no, setting boundaries, being physically active, being kind to yourself, getting off social media, managing your stress—the list is endless!

For me, self-care and self-love have been a journey. As many of you probably can relate to, I am often ruthless with myself, holding myself to impossibly high standards and pushing my mind, body, and calendar to the extremes as I seek to do the work that I find both fulfilling and necessary. Through the writing of this book and deepening my own relationship with Chicana feminism, I have learned that if we are to do the work necessary to change engineering and computing environments for Latina students, we must do it at full capacity. If you, like me, find yourself at times depleted and in need of self-care and love, here are a few of the books I have found helpful on my journey:

- *Chingona: Owning Your Inner Badass for Healing and Justice* by Alma Zaragoza-Petty
- *For Brown Girls with Sharp Edges and Tender Hearts: A Love Letter to Women of Color* by Prisca Dorcas Mojica Rodriguez
- *Woman Who Glows in the Dark: A Curandera Reveals Traditional Aztec Secrets of Physical and Spiritual Health* by Elena Avila (with Joy Parker)
- *Self-Love for Latinas: Unveiling Your Inner Strength | How to Be Kind to Yourself | Heal from the Childhood Trauma, That's Holding You Back | Nurturing Self-Compassion Amidst Life's Trials* by Rosario Alvarez
- *Self-Care for Latinas: 100+ Ways to Prioritize and Rejuvenate Your Mind, Body, and Spirit* by Raquel Reichard

Now, beyond the individual, a Chicana feminist approach to self-care and love also **focuses on collective care, rather than relying solely on individual acts of care**. I know we just talked about individual self-care and love, but we must also support and uplift each other as well as celebrate our identities, knowing that our experiences are inherently of value and deserving of respect. Collective care can come in many forms (e.g., book clubs, professional organizations, support groups) and be any group, big or small, that you believe will pour strength into you and that you can contribute something to. It is within these collectives that solidarity is created, experiences are shared, and souls are strengthened for the continued battle ahead.

CONCLUSION

As I said before, when I first started writing this book, there was no resistance chapter. And although ostensibly you could do the work of enhancing engineering and computing identity for Latina students without a discussion of resistance, the work would not be the same. Part of what it means to take a Chicana feminist approach is, without a doubt, rooted in the act of pushing toward liberation and empowerment. This chapter focused on how to engage in resistance to nurture engineering and computing identity for Latina students. From this standpoint, I discussed what it means to reconcile *la nepantlera* with the engineering and computing identity context and how we might make space for reflection and critical consciousness building. I also addressed how work as equity-minded practitioners might be enhanced by confronting the whiteness in our efforts as well as how we might transform engineering and computing identity through spiritual activism. In the next chapter, I explore what it means to harness our collective power toward a collective, multipronged approach to enhancing engineering and computing identity for Latina students.

CHAPTER 8

Working Together

How Institutions Can Facilitate a Collective, Multipronged Approach to Enhancing Engineering and Computing Identity for Latina Students

We must act in the everyday world. Words are not enough. We must perform visible and public acts that may make us more vulnerable to the very oppressions we are fighting against. But, our vulnerability can be the source of our power—if we use it. . . . The vision of radical Third World Feminism necessitates our willingness to work with those people who would feel at home in El Mundo Zurdo, the left-handed world: the colored, the queer, the poor, the female, the physically challenged. . . . The change evoked on these pages is material as well as psychic. Change requires a lot of heat. It requires both the alchemist and the welder, the magician and the laborer, the witch and the warrior, the myth-smasher and the myth-maker. Hand in Hand, we brew and forge a revolution.

–Cherríe Moraga and Gloria Anzaldúa[1]

When practitioners ask me for the magic bullet to address engineering and computing identity for Latina students, I am always at a loss. There is no one method or action, no one relationship or form of resistance that will solve the deeply entrenched problems that exist. There is no magical formula for promoting engineering and computing identity and no one-size-fits-all approach that will meet the needs of all institutions, all Latina students, or all engineering and computing contexts. Likewise, there is no one group—faculty, advising and support practitioners, leaders, or Latina students and their communities—who can, alone, address these issues. It is only through working together, on all fronts, that we can hope to enhance engineering and computing identity for Latina college students.

My vision for enhancing engineering and computing identity for Latina students is similar in many ways to *El Mundo Zũrdo* advocated by Moraga and Anzaldúa. It is through collective action and engagement from a wide range of individuals and groups engaging not only in dialogue but also in action that we will achieve better results. To fully embody this vision requires practitioners to adopt an integrated, asset-based approach to engineering and computing identity that draws upon Chicana feminist approaches to radically rethink how we think and act. Chicana feminism offers a framework for understanding and addressing the experiences and challenges of Latina engineering and computing students. By incorporating these principles, engineering educators can help create an educational environment that is supportive, empowering, and inclusive for Latina students in engineering and computing. We must focus our efforts and come together to revolutionize the way that we think about engineering and computing identity and be resolute in forging ahead with a multipronged approach to change. This is hard work, but it is worth the effort to see generations of Latina engineers and computer scientists benefit across the nation.

WHY A COLLECTIVE MULTIPRONGED APPROACH?

Rather than relying on a single approach to encouraging engineering and computing identity development, this chapter outlines the need for a collective, multipronged approach that addresses change across several practitioner areas: teaching, advising and support, and leadership (see figure 8.1). Being part of

FIGURE 8.1. How institutions can facilitate a collective, multipronged approach to enhancing engineering and computing identity for Latina students

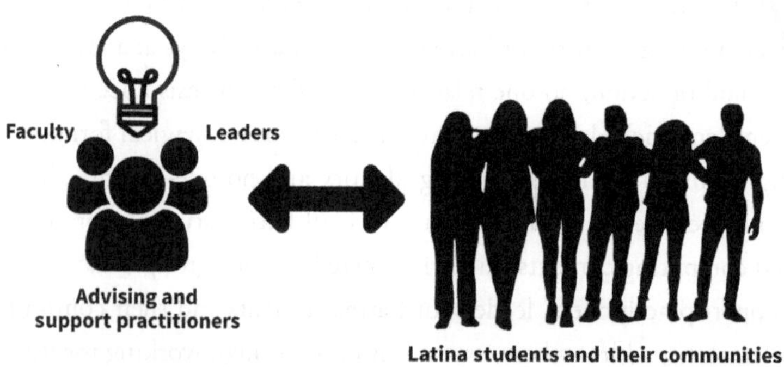

a collective implies working together, moving in unison with a shared vision, coordinated efforts, and a common commitment to enhancing engineering and computing identity for Latina students. It is imperative not to shy away from acting and collaborating across diverse groups, sectors, institutions, and programs. Fear of making mistakes, falling short, or not achieving perfection should not deter us from action. Bringing about change demands resolute and unambiguous steps on multiple fronts. This approach enables equity-minded practitioners across the institution not only to have a shared vision for enhancing Latina student experiences but also to see that vision followed through.

Chicana feminism invites us to step into consciousness to serve students. This means promoting identity development within and outside of the classroom by investigating the teaching and curriculum as well as the advising and support changes needed to support Latina students in these fields. In addition, this means empowering college leaders to act as catalysts of change and community building in order to facilitate a multipronged approach to enhancing engineering and computing identity for Latina students.

The Importance of Faculty Members for Student Identity

Equity-minded faculty members have the ability to directly influence the identity experiences of Latina students in these fields because they are involved with the day-to-day teaching and curriculum design and delivery. Teaching and curriculum design have an explicit impact on engineering and computing identity. It's important to remember that teaching, or the process of facilitating learning and the acquisition of knowledge, skills, values, beliefs, and attitudes in others, takes many forms and occurs in different settings, including classrooms, online, seminars, and mentoring contexts, among many more. Good teaching requires a commitment to student learning and development and can empower Latina students to become lifelong learners who contribute to society in meaningful ways. Curriculum design, or the process of structuring educational experiences, requires a deep understanding of engineering and computing, as well as familiarity with a range of effective teaching techniques and approaches for these fields done at scale. Well-designed engineering and computing curricula create strong foundational knowledge and inspire innovation, creativity, and social responsibility. Together, teaching and curriculum can be thought of as a process of becoming in which Latina students take up and refine their engineering and computing identities. These elements set the tone of the field and shape how Latina students are socialized to become an engineering or computing person. Teaching and curriculum are constantly under scrutiny and attack because society recognizes that these are influential, dynamic, and transformational spaces. Such attacks seek to restrict Latina students from fully and authentically seeing themselves in roles as engineers or computer scientists and, ultimately, constrain their success.

As equity-minded practitioners, you should seek to identify strategies to address Latina students' engineering and computing identity through your own teaching and the curriculum. You might begin thinking of the engineering or computing journey as a process of coming to be and come to understand the importance of building, refining, and maintaining an engineering and computing identity. Faculty can shape curricula around identity, including structuring experiences that encourage building interests and competence and providing opportunities for identity performance and recognition, which, for many Latina students, may have been stifled by prior marginalization within engineering and computing environments. Faculty can cultivate environments in which these identities can be nurtured. For example, faculty members might look to ways in which students can follow their interests with assignments and build competence in areas that excite them or appeal to their long-term goals. In addition, faculty can also look for ways in which Latina students can take on the role of an engineer or computer scientist through hands-on, real-life learning experiences that encourage them to apply their knowledge and skills, especially in front of others.

The Importance of Advising and Support Practitioners in Developing Identity

Equity-minded advising and support practitioners drive transformational change. Often this work goes unseen and unrecognized, but nonetheless, it is foundational to ensuring that students succeed, especially those historically marginalized by the education system. Over the years, it has been the advising and support practitioners who have reached out to me with questions about how we translate key ideas about engineering and computing identity into practice. Your questions, your desires, and your commitment are what keep me dedicated to doing this work in so many ways. Reflecting on our team's research, I see that Latina students in engineering and computing also recognize the important role that advising and support practitioners play in building and sustaining their identities. They speak to the ability of equity-minded practitioners, like you, to guide them through developing their interests and competence as well as to provide opportunities for performing and being recognized as engineers and computer scientists.

Advising and other support services can be structured and executed to encourage engineering and computing identity for Latina students. Practitioners within support offices may often be the first individuals Latina students encounter on their engineering and computing journeys. As such, it is important that those working in these offices and on initiatives understand their role in shaping engineering and computing identity. You can create integrated approaches to encourage engineering and computing identity for Latinas. Rather than working in isolation, you should consider how various advising and support strategies might be redefined around a common vision for enhancing engineering and computing identity. That common vision can bring together ideas for how support services, relationship building, and resistance efforts can work together toward a more inclusive and identity-forward learning environment. As equity-minded practitioners, you might advocate for support services that work with internal and external partners to build engineering and computing identities, including looking for ways for advising and support staff to be meaningfully integrated with others focused on building identity (e.g., faculty, leaders, Latina students and their communities).

The Importance of Leaders in Developing Identity

As change agents, higher education leaders are guides, not only to their colleagues but also to the students and broader communities they serve. You might have felt called to become a leader because of your deeply held beliefs and values or a desire to resist forms of oppression and shift the engineering and computing cultures around you. As leaders, you assume roles in which you possess influence and a responsibility for managing change, but that's not where your work ends. You also shine a light into the darkness, encouraging your institutions to venture into uncharted territories. Whether or not you are a member of the Latin* community, by picking up this book, you have moved toward making an investment as a leader who seeks to act as a bridge between Latin* communities and higher education institutions.

Institutional leaders can be catalysts for change in shaping engineering and computing identity-informed practices and policies as well as creating partnerships with communities and industry. Leaders must consider the identity process as they craft the structural and systematic ways in which Latina students experience their educational journeys. To do so, leaders must gain an understanding of the institutional landscape of the engineering and computing curricula and programs to avoid duplication, identify gaps, and propose new partnerships and strategies to address challenges and opportunities for identity. They must review existing activities and policies to determine if they are serving an agenda to enhance engineering and computing identity, especially for marginalized populations like Latina students. These efforts should leverage expertise and resources to make a collective impact on the engineering and computing identity of Latina students by coordinating multiple programs, initiatives, and services that will have a greater effect than a single strategy alone. Furthermore, leaders should identify federal, foundation, and industry funding to support the work that furthers establishing identity during the college experience.

The Importance of Latina Students and Their Communities

Although it should be evident by this point in the book that I consider Latina students and their communities to be essential to enhancing engineering and computing identity, I would be remiss if I did not explicitly acknowledge them as integral to the multiprong approach laid out here. Latina students bring with them a wealth of knowledge and experiences that can bring insight to creating a more identity-forward set of strategies for improving engineering and computing identity. As individuals, Latina students bring with them their own experiences and ways of knowing derived from their home and greater communities. As a group, Latina students represent a rich pool of engineering and computing talent that cannot be ignored. Similarly, Latin* communities offer cultural wealth, collective strength, and care that so often are overlooked. Rather than creating expansive borderlands between engineering and computing fields and Latin* communities, equity-minded practitioners should seek to make those borders more fluid and permeable. Doing so will enable Latina students in these fields to see themselves and their communities reflected in the aims and mission of the institution and feel more able to bring their whole selves to the educational process.

Involving Latina students in engineering and computing and their communities takes time, commitment, and a willingness to invest beyond mere outreach, enrollment, or graduation. It requires equity-minded practitioners to truly value the contributions and ways of knowing of the Latin* communities and create meaningful strategies for how to involve them in multiple areas of the engineering and computing identity journey.

CONCLUSION AND NEXT STEPS

This book encapsulates a journey of exploration, discovery, and advocacy toward enhancing engineering and computing identity for Latina students. It reflects on the transformative power of nurturing engineering and computing identity, fueled by the perspectives of Chicana feminism, critical consciousness, community building, and resistance against oppressive structures. It acknowledges the complexities of identity formation, the importance of diverse perspectives, and the need to tailor interventions to contextual realities. Moreover, it leaves a trail of opportunities for collaboration and intervention, echoing a commitment to fostering equitable and inclusive pathways within the domains of engineering and computing.

It is my hope that the book leaves you with the desire and inspiration to do the work of resisting the many forms of oppression that exist for our Latina college students, even during times, like those we live in today, where resistance feels incredibly difficult. It is the duty of all of us to carry our responsibilities with both dignity and strength. And while I do not envy the challenging and complex decisions that you, as leaders, are forced to make on a daily basis, I hope you know that every day I send my love to all of you, wishing that you know that your investment toward enhancing identity for Latina students in engineering and computing aids a worthy, honored, and respected cause, with far larger implications than even you or I can imagine. It is my desire that in this book you have found a sense of pride and inspiration in what your institution is doing to facilitate identity for Latina engineering and computing students and that you are inspired to keep pushing toward greater means of enhancement. But the work is not done. We should continue delving into the engineering and computing identity experiences of Latina students and working toward enhancing the process of becoming. Together, I believe that we can move on many fronts, including a greater push toward a research-to-practice model and activating faculty, advising and support practitioners, and leaders throughout the nation to rethink engineering and computing identity using Chicana feminism as a guide.

As you, an equity-minded practitioner, consider next steps for yourself and your institutions, I suggest a few places to start with your multipronged approach to enhancing the engineering and computing identity experiences of Latina students:

- **Know your context:** You cannot begin to facilitate a multipronged approach unless you know the classroom, institutional, and societal contexts in which your work will take place. Knowing this context is important to all involved in order to get a more accurate picture of the areas in which your institution is doing well and the areas in which your institution might improve their approaches to enhancing engineering and computing identity for Latina students. Interactions with Latina students and Latin* communities are hallmark to knowing your context and serving key needs.
- **Find your people:** A multipronged approach does not work without a clear tie between the prongs of that approach. Finding your collaborators can be tricky, but identifying who in your networks cares about the identity experiences of Latina students and how each of you might contribute to the enhancement of these experiences is vital. Your people do not necessarily have to be at your institution; reach out to Latin* organizations, community partners, and colleagues at other institutions who can galvanize your ability to enhance engineering and computing identity for Latina students.
- **Create a shared vision:** Once you find your people, creating a shared vision of what enhancing engineering and computing identity might look like is key. Although there are many guiding principles and strategies presented in this book, one institution or group of collaborators cannot possibly address all of them, nor will these institutions or groups all have the same idea of what it means to enhance engineering and computing identity. People are in different stages of their understanding and come from vastly different standpoints and responsibilities, so it is your job as equity-minded practitioners to consider what elements are essential in the shared vision for creating change.
- **Create a blueprint for action:** Finally, you will want to create a blueprint for action. With a shared vision established, the creation of a blueprint for action can guide and align efforts across the multipronged approach.

> Rather than going in many different directions, a blueprint for action focuses the multipronged approach and increases the likelihood that Latina students in engineering and computing will be served in meaningful ways. As always, the blueprint for action must include the various groups laid out in this chapter—faculty, advising and support practitioners, leaders, Latina students, and Latin* communities—for a greater, positive impact on engineering and computing identity.

It is my hope that in the future equity-minded practitioners might use this book as a tool to outline a multipronged approach to engineering and computing identity and engage in dialogue, planning, and actions to enhance the process of becoming. Students need this process of becoming to feel a sense of connectedness and validation between themselves and their careers. It is our responsibility to meet those needs. I envision a world in which Latina students can truly bring their whole selves into these learning environments and become the kinds of engineers and computer scientists that *they want to become.*

Notes

Preface

1. Gloria Anzaldúa, "Speaking in Tongues: A Letter to 3rd World Women Writers," in *This Bridge Called My Back: Writings by Radical Women of Color*, ed. Cherríe Moraga and Gloria Anzaldúa, 4th ed. (New York: State University of New York Press, 2015), 168–69.
2. S. L. Laursen, *Levers for Change: An Assessment of Progress on Changing STEM Instruction* (Washington, DC: American Association of the Advancement of Science, 2019), https://www.aaas.org/sites/default/files/2019-07/levers-for-change-WEB100_2019.pdf.

Chapter 1

1. Gloria Anzaldúa, *Light in the Dark/Luz en lo Oscuro: Rewriting Identity, Spirituality, Reality*, ed. AnaLouise Keating (Durham, NC: Duke University Press, 2015).
2. See, for example, Estela Mara Bensimon et al., "The Role of Institutional Agents in Providing Institutional Support to Latinx Students in STEM," *Review of Higher Education* 42, no. 4 (2019): 16891–721; Megan Michaelene Chase, Estela Bensimon, and Jason Robinson, "The Implementation of a Large-Scale Pathway Reform: How Department Chairs Make Sense of and Navigate a Pathway Initiative in a Community College," *Community College Journal of Research and Practice* 45, no. 9 (2021): 631–48; Megan Michaelene Chase et al., "Constraints and Opportunities for Practitioner Agency in STEM Programs in Hispanic Serving Community Colleges," in *Community Colleges and STEM* (New York: Routledge, 2013), 192–212; Mays Imad, "Trauma-Informed Education for Wholeness: Strategies for Faculty and Advisors," *New Directions for Student Services* 177 (2022): 39–47.
3. I use the term Latin* to refer to anyone who identifies as Latina/o/x/e; this community is made up of individuals from or having origins in Latin America and is gender expansive in nature.
4. *Hispanic Americans' Trust in and Engagement with Science* (Washington, DC: Pew Research Center, 2022), https://www.pewresearch.org/science/2022/06/14/a-brief-statistical-portrait-of-u-s-hispanics/.
5. National Center for Science and Engineering Statistics (NCSES), *Diversity and STEM: Women, Minorities, and Persons with Disabilities 2023* (Alexandria, VA: National Science Foundation, 2023), https://ncses.nsf.gov/wmpd.
6. NCSES, *Diversity and STEM.*
7. E. L. Anderson et al., *The 2018 Status Report on Engineering Education: A Snapshot of Diversity in Degrees Conferred in Engineering* (Washington, DC: Association of Public and Land-Grant Universities, 2018); F. McAlear et al., *Women and Girls of Color in Computing* (Tempe: Arizona State University, Kapor Center, 2018), https://www.wocincomputing.org/#data-brief.
8. Stephen Secules, "Making the Familiar Strange: An Ethnographic Scholarship of Integration Contextualizing Engineering Educational Culture as Masculine and Competitive," *Engineering Studies* 11, no. 3 (2019): 196–216, https://doi.org/10.1080/19378629.2019.1663200.

9. *Oxford English Dictionary*, "Engineer, n," https://www.oed.com/dictionary/engineer_n.
10. *Oxford English Dictionary*, "Computing," https://www.oed.com/dictionary/computing_n.
11. K. J. Jensen et al., "Undergraduate Student Perceptions of Stress and Mental Health in Engineering Culture," *International Journal of STEM Education* 10, no. 1 (2023): 30.
12. A. True-Funk et al., "Intersectional Engineers: Diversity of Gender and Race Microaggressions and Their Effects in Engineering Education," *Journal of Management in Engineering* 37, no. 3 (2021): 04021002, https://doi.org/10.1061/(ASCE)ME.1943-5479.0000889.
13. P. O. Garriott et al., "How Latiné Engineering Students Resist White Male Engineering Culture: A Multi-Institution Analysis of Academic Engagement," *Journal of Engineering Education* 112, no. 3 (2023): 695–718, https://doi.org/10.1002/jee.20536.
14. S. Brooke, "Breaking Gender Code: Visibility, Power, and Gender in Creative Coding Cultures" (PhD diss., University of Oxford, 2020); E. Chang, *Brotopia: Breaking Up the Boys' Club of Silicon Valley* (New York: Penguin, 2019).
15. E. R. McCurdy, "Discrimination as a Barrier to Diversity: Sexism and Microaggressions Against African American Women in Computer Science and Engineering" (PhD diss, University of Akron, 2020); K. C. Smith et al., "Ethnicity, Race, and Gender in Engineering Education: The Nuanced Experiences of Male and Female Latinx Engineering Undergraduates Targeted by Microaggressions," *Psychological Reports* 126, no. 5 (2023): 2345–82.
16. J. Lopez et al., "What Is a Computer Scientist? Unpacking the Ontological Beliefs of Black and Hispanic Female Computing Students," in *Proceedings of the 53rd ACM Technical Symposium on Computer Science Education-Volume 1* (2022): 369–75.
17. S. L. Rodriguez, C. Lu, and D. Ramirez, "Creating a Conceptual Framework for Computing Identity Development for Latina Undergraduate Students," in *An Asset-Based Approach to Advancing Latina Students in STEM: Increasing Resilience, Participation, and Success*, ed. Elsa Gonzalez, Frank Fernandez, and Miranda Wilson (New York: Routledge, 2020), 25.
18. W. C. Lee and S. L. Rodriguez, "Reimagining STEM Higher Education Research: Issue 1 of 2," *Journal of Women and Minorities in Science and Engineering* 28, no. 2 (2022), https://doi.org/10.1615/JWomenMinorScienEng.2022042358; S. L. Rodriguez and W. C. Lee, "Reimagining STEM Higher Education Research: Issue 2 of 2," *Journal of Women and Minorities in Science and Engineering* 28, no. 3 (2022), https://doi.org/10.1615/JWomenMinorScienEng.2022042359.
19. Gloria Anzaldúa, *Borderlands, La Frontera: The New Mestiza* (San Francisco: Aunt Lute Books, 1987); Gloria Anzaldúa and Cherríe Moraga, eds., *This Bridge Called My Back: Writings by Radical Women of Color* (Watertown, MA: Persephone, 1981).
20. M. M. Camacho and S. M. Lord, *The Borderlands of Education: Latinas in Engineering* (Lanham, MD: Lexington Books, 2013).
21. G. Q. Conchas and N. Acevedo, *The Chicana/o/x Dream: Hope, Resistance, and Educational Success* (Boston: Harvard Education Press, 2020).
22. A. Hurtado, *Voicing Chicana Feminisms: Young Women Speak Out on Sexuality and Identity*, vol. 1 (New York: New York University Press, 2003).
23. Anzaldúa and Moraga, *This Bridge.*
24. M. Baca Zinn and R. E. Zambrana, "Chicanas/Latinas Advance Intersectional Thought and Practice," *Gender and Society* 33, no. 5 (2019): 677–701.
25. J. A. Mejia et al., "Critical Theoretical Frameworks in Engineering Education: An Anti-Deficit and Liberative Approach," *Education Sciences* 8, no. 4 (2018): 158; L. I. Rendón et al., "Científicos Latinxs: Uncovering the Counter-Story of Success in STEM," in *High-Achieving Latino Students: Successful Pathways Toward College and Beyond*, ed. S. J.

Paik et al. (Charlotte, NC: Information Age Publishing, 2019), 159–77; S. L. Rodriguez, C. Lu, and D. Ramirez, "Navigating Operating Systems: A Framework for Understanding Identity Development for Undergraduate Latina Students in Computing," in *An Asset-Based Approach to Advancing Latina Students in STEM: Increasing Resilience, Participation, and Success*, ed. E. M. Gonzalez, F. Fernandez, and M. Wilson (London: Routledge, 2020); S. L. Rodriguez et al., "Critiquing Oppression and Desiring Social Justice: How Undergraduate Latinas in STEM Engage in Acts of Resistance," *NASPA Journal of Women and Gender in Higher Education* 13, no. 3 (2020): 251–67, https://doi.org/10.1080/26379112.2020.1838297; S. L. Rodriguez et al., "Utilizing Community Cultural Wealth to Explore the Experiences of Latina Undergraduate Students in Computing," *Journal of Women and Minorities in Science and Engineering* 29, no. 3 (2023): 1–24, https://doi.org/10.1615/JWomenMinorScienEng.2022039365.

26. S. L. Rodriguez and N. Garza, "The Promise and Future of Latinas in STEM," *Hispanic Outlook on Education Magazine*, May 2022, https://www.hispanicoutlook.com/articles/unicorns-no-more.
27. M. R. Kendall et al., "Factors Influencing Engineering Identity Development of Latinx Students," *IEEE Transactions on Education* 62, no. 3 (2019): 173–80, https://doi.org/10.1109/TE.2019.2909857; S. L. Rodriguez et al., "Becoming la Ingeniera: Examining the Engineering Identity Development of Undergraduate Latina Students," *Journal of Latinos and Education* 21, no. 2 (2022): 181–200.
28. A. Esquinca, E. Mein, and H. Mucino, "Latinx Students' Sense of Belonging in Engineering/Computer Science at an HSI" (paper presented at the Collaborative Network for Engineering and Computing Diversity Virtual Conference, January 24–28, 2021), https://strategy.asee.org/36105; L. Y. Flores et al., "Social Cognitive Predictors of Latinx and White Engineering Students' Academic Satisfaction and Persistence Intentions: Exploring Interactions Among Social Identities and Institutional Context," *Journal of Vocational Behavior* 127 (2021): 103580, https://doi.org/10.1016/j.jvb.2021.103580; J. A. Mejia et al., "Legitimized Tongues: Breaking the Traditions of Silence in Mainstream Engineering Education and Research," *Journal of Women and Minorities in Science and Engineering* 28, no. 2 (2022): 53–77, https://doi.org/10.1615/JWomenMinorScienEng.2022036603; E. Turochy et al., "Types of Stereotype Threats That Latinx Students Experience in Undergraduate Engineering Education" (paper presented at American Society for Engineering Education Virtual Annual Conference, July 26–29, 2021), https://peer.asee.org/types-of-stereotype-threats-that-latinx-students-experience-in-undergraduate-engineering-education-research.pdf.
29. E. Mein et al., "Building a Pathway to Engineering: The Influence of Family and Teachers Among Mexican-Origin Undergraduate Engineering Students," *Journal of Hispanic Higher Education* 19, no. 1 (2020): 37–51, https://doi.org/10.1177/1538192718772082; R. A. Revelo and L. D. Baber, "Engineering Resistors: Engineering Latina/o Students and Emerging Resistant Capital," *Journal of Hispanic Higher Education* 17, no. 3 (2017): 249–69, https://doi.org/10.1177/1538192717719132; H. E. Rodríguez-Simmonds, "Transcending the Margins and Boundaries as Latin-American Engineer," in *Queering STEM Culture in U.S. Higher Education*, ed. K. J. Cross, S. Farrell, and B. Hughes (New York: Routledge, 2022), 36–56.
30. Secules, "Making the Familiar Strange"; S. L. Rodriguez and K. Lehman, "Developing the Next Generation of Diverse Computer Scientists: The Need for Enhanced, Intersectional Computing Identity Theory," *Computer Science Education* 27, no. 3–4 (2017): 229–47, https://doi.org/10.1080/08993408.2018.1457899.

31. H. B. Carlone and A. Johnson, "Understanding the Science Experiences of Successful Women of Color: Science Identity as an Analytic Lens," *Journal of Research in Science Teaching* 44, no. 8 (2007): 1187–218, https://doi.org/10.1002/tea.20237.
32. M. Ong et al., "Inside the Double Bind: A Synthesis of Empirical Research on Undergraduate and Graduate Women of Color in Science, Technology, Engineering, and Mathematics," *Harvard Educational Review* 81, no. 2 (2011): 172–208, https://doi.org/10.17763/haer.81.2.t022245n7x4752v2.
33. K. Crenshaw, "Mapping the Margins: Intersectionality, Identity Politics, and Violence Against Women of Color," *Stanford Law Review* 43, no. 6 (1991): 1241–99, https://doi.org/10.2307/1229039.
34. K. J. Cross et al., "The Double Bind of Race and Gender: A Look into the Experiences of Women of Color in Engineering" (paper presented at the American Society of Engineering Education Annual Conference and Exposition, Columbus, OH, June 24–28, 2017); H. K. Ro and K. I. Loya, "The Effect of Gender and Race Intersectionality on Student Learning Outcomes in Engineering," *Review of Higher Education* 38, no. 3 (2015): 359–96.
35. T. J. Yosso, "Whose Culture Has Capital? A Critical Race Theory Discussion of Community Cultural Wealth," *Race Ethnicity and Education* 8, no. 1 (2005): 69–91; Moises Esteban-Guitart and Luis C. Moll, "Funds of Identity: A New Concept Based on the Funds of Knowledge Approach," *Culture and Psychology* 20, no. 1 (2014): 31–48; K. W. Crenshaw, "Mapping the Margins: Intersectionality, Identity Politics, and Violence Against Women of Color," in *The Public Nature of Private Violence*, ed. Martha Albertson Fineman (New York: Routledge, 2013), 93–118.
36. J. O. Thomas et al., "Speaking Truth to Power: Exploring the Intersectional Experiences of Black Women in Computing," *2018 Research on Equity and Sustained Participation in Engineering, Computing, and Technology (RESPECT)* (2018): 1–8, https://doi.org/10.1109/RESPECT.2018.8491718; T. C. Madkins et al., "Culturally Relevant Computer Science Pedagogy: From Theory to Practice," *2019 Research on Equity and Sustained Participation in Engineering, Computing, and Technology (RESPECT)* (2019): 1–4, https://doi.org/10.1109/RESPECT46404.2019.8985773; K. A. Scott, K. M. Sheridan, and K. Clark, "Culturally Responsive Computing: A Theory Revisited," *Learning, Media and Technology* 40, no. 4 (2015): 412–36.
37. N. E. Cantù, "Getting There Cuando No Hay Camino (When There Is No Path): Paths to Discovery Testimonios by Chicanas in STEM," *Equity and Excellence in Education* 45, no. 3 (2012): 472–87, https://doi.org/10.1080/10665684.2012.698936; D. G. Solórzano and D. Delgado Bernal, "Examining Transformational Resistance Through a Critical Race and Latcrit Theory Framework: Chicana and Chicano Students in an Urban Context," *Urban Education* 36, no. 3 (2001): 308–42, https://doi.org/10.1177/0042085901363002.
38. R. M. Banda, "From the Inside Looking Out: Latinas Intersectionality and Their Engineering Departments," *International Journal of Qualitative Studies in Education* 33, no. 8 (2020): 824–39; E. Q. Villa et al., "'Is Engineering for Me?': Examining Latinas' Narratives of Resilience and Agency to Confront Enduring Struggles and Challenges in Undergraduate Engineering Studies," *Peace and Conflict: Journal of Peace Psychology* 26, no. 4 (2020): 403–13, https://doi.org/10.1037/pac0000427.
39. S. L. Rodriguez et al., "Becoming La Ingeniera: Examining the Engineering Identity Development of Undergraduate Latinas," *Journal of Latinos in Education* 21, no. 2 (2022): 181–200, https://doi.org/10.1080/15348431.2019.1648269.

40. National Center for Science and Engineering Statistics, *Women, Minorities, and Persons with Disabilities in Science and Engineering: 2021*, Special Report NSF 21-321 (Alexandria, VA: National Science Foundation, 2021), https://ncses.nsf.gov/wmpd.
41. Rodriguez et al., "Creating a Conceptual Framework," 25.
42. Enrique López et al., "Latinx Students' Sense of *Familismo* in Undergraduate Science and Engineering," *Review of Higher Education* 43, no. 1 (2019): 85–111.
43. Madkins et al., "Culturally Relevant Computer Science Pedagogy"; E. McGee and L. Bentley, "The Equity Ethic: Black and Latinx College Students Reengineering Their STEM Careers Toward Justice," *American Journal of Education* 124, no. 1 (2017): 1–36.
44. Sharin Rawhiya Jacob, Jonathan Montoya, and Mark Warschauer, "Exploring the Intersectional Development of Computer Science Identities in Young Latinas," *Teachers College Record* 124, no. 5 (2022): 166–85; S. L. Rodriguez et al., "Becoming La Ingeniera: Examining the Engineering Identity Development of Undergraduate Latina Students," *Journal of Latinos and Education* 21, no. 2 (2022): 181–200.
45. Rodriguez et al., "Utilizing Community Cultural Wealth"; T. J. Yosso, "Whose Culture Has Capital? A Critical Race Theory Discussion of Community Cultural Wealth," *Race Ethnicity and Education* 8, no. 1 (2005): 69–91.
46. S. L. Rodriguez et al., "Inclusion and Marginalization: How Perceptions of Design Thinking Pedagogy Influence Computer, Electrical, and Software Engineering Identity," *International Journal of Education in Mathematics, Science and Technology* 8, no. 4 (2020): 304–17.
47. Rodriguez et al., "Creating a Conceptual Framework."
48. Mein et al., "Building a Pathway to Engineering"; Esquinca et al., "Latinx Students' Sense of Belonging."
49. S. L. Rodriguez and J. M. Blaney, "'We're the Unicorns in STEM': Understanding How Academic and Social Experiences Influence Sense of Belonging for Latina Undergraduate Students," *Journal of Diversity in Higher Education* 14, no. 3 (2021): 441–55, https://doi.org/10.1037/dhe0000176.
50. Rodriguez et al., "Critiquing Oppression."

Chapter 2

1. Gloria Anzaldúa, *Light in the Dark/Luz en lo Oscuro: Rewriting Identity, Spirituality, Reality*, ed. AnaLouise Keating (Durham, NC: Duke University Press, 2015).
2. Shaun R. Harper, "An Anti-Deficit Achievement Framework for Research on Students of Color in STEM," *New Directions for Institutional Research 2010*, no. 148 (2010): 63–74.
3. Moises Esteban-Guitart and Luis C. Moll, "Funds of Identity: A New Concept Based on the Funds of Knowledge Approach," *Culture and Psychology* 20 (2014): 31–48; S. L. Rodriguez et al., "Utilizing Community Cultural Wealth to Explore the Experiences of Latina Undergraduate Students in Computing," *Journal of Women and Minorities in Science and Engineering* 29, no. 3 (2023): 1–24, https://doi.org/10.1615/JWomenMinorScienEng.2022039365; T. J. Yosso, "Whose Culture Has Capital? A Critical Race Theory Discussion of Community Cultural Wealth," *Race Ethnicity and Education* 8, no. 1 (2005): 69–91.
4. Yosso, "Whose Culture Has Capital?"
5. Anzaldúa, *Light in the Dark*, 69.
6. Aída Hurtado, *Voicing Chicana Feminisms: Young Women Speak Out on Sexuality and Identity* (New York: New York University Press, 2003), 261.

7. Gloria E. Anzaldúa, "Writing a Way of Life: An Interview with María Henríquez Betancor," in *Interviews/Entrevistas* (New York: Routledge, 2020), 238.
8. Anzaldúa, *Light in the Dark*, 66.
9. Gloria Anzaldúa, "A Way of Life: An Interview with María Henríquez Betancor (1995)," in *Interviews/Entrevistas* (New York: Routledge, 2000), 111.
10. Anzaldúa, *Light in the Dark*, 135.
11. Anzaldúa, *Light in the Dark*, 69.
12. Anzaldúa, *Light in the Dark*, 75.
13. Anzaldúa, *Light in the Dark*, 118.

Chapter 3

1. Gloria Anzaldúa, "Foreword to the Second Edition," in *This Bridge Called My Back, Fortieth Anniversary Edition: Writings by Radical Women of Color*, ed. Cherríe Moraga and Gloria Anzaldúa (Albany: State University of New York Press, 2021).
2. C. Van Haren and D. Friedman, *Transitions* (Charlotte, NC: National Resource Center for the First-Year Experience and Students in Transition, 2018).
3. S. L. Rodriguez, C. Lu, and D. Ramirez, "Creating a Conceptual Framework for Computing Identity Development for Latina Undergraduate Students," in *An Asset-Based Approach to Advancing Latina Students in STEM: Increasing Resilience, Participation, and Success*, ed. Elsa Gonzalez, Frank Fernandez, and Miranda Wilson (New York: Routledge, 2020), 25.
4. See, for example, S. L. Rodriguez, "Las Mujeres in the STEM Pipeline: How Latina College Students Who Persist in STEM Majors Develop and Sustain Their Science Identities" (PhD diss., 2015); Sarah L. Rodriguez, Erin E. Doran, Mackenzie Sissel, and Nia Estes, "Becoming la Ingeniera: Examining the Engineering Identity Development of Undergraduate Latina Students," *Journal of Latinos and Education* 21, no. 2 (2022): 181–200.
5. S. Rodriguez, K. Cunningham, and A. Jordan, "STEM Identity Development for Latinas: The Role of Self-and Outside Recognition," *Journal of Hispanic Higher Education* 18, no. 3 (2019): 254–72.
6. Rodriguez et al., "STEM Identity Development for Latinas."
7. Rodriguez et al., "STEM Identity Development for Latinas"; S. Rodriguez, A. Pilcher, and N. Garcia-Tellez, "The Influence of *Familismo* on Latina Student STEM Identity Development," *Journal of Latinos and Education* 20, no. 2 (2021): 177–89.
8. Daisy Ramirez et al., "'I Started Seeing Myself as a Computing Person': Exploring Latina Women's Computing Identity Development in College," *Journal Committed to Social Change on Race and Ethnicity* 10, no. 2 (2024): 24–43.
9. Society of Women Engineers, accessed December 20, 2024, https://swe.org/.
10. Rodriguez et al., "Becoming la Ingeniera."
11. Rodriguez, "Las Mujeres in the STEM Pipeline"; Rodriguez et al., "STEM Identity Development for Latinas."

Chapter 4

1. R. Flores, "The New Chicana and Machismo," in *Chicana Feminist Thought: The Basic Historical Writings*, ed. A. Garcia (New York: Routledge, 1997).
2. S. L. Rodriguez and A. R. Stevens, "Exploring Computing Identity Development for Latinx Students at a Hispanic-Serving Community College," *Journal of Diversity in Higher Education* (2023), https://doi.org/10.1037/dhe0000530; S. L. Rodriguez et al., "Becoming

la Ingeniera: Examining the Engineering Identity Development of Undergraduate Latina Students," *Journal of Latinos and Education* 21, no. 2 (2022): 181–200.

3. K. J. C. Espinoza and B. E. Rincón, "Color-Evasive/Conscious? A Content Analysis of How Engineering Faculty Discuss Race and Racism in a U.S.-Based Equity-Focused STEM Professional Development Program," *Education Sciences* 13, no. 3 (2023): 233, https://doi.org/10.3390/educsci13030233; K. A. Scott and P. Garcia, "Techno-Social Change Agents: Fostering Activist Dispositions Among Girls of Color," *Meridians: Feminism, Race, Transnationalism* 15, no. 1 (2016): 65–85.
4. S. L. Rodriguez and A. Kaur, "Understanding Latina Computing Identity Development at a Hispanic-Serving Community College" (paper presented at Association for the Study of Higher Education Annual Conference, Minneapolis, MN, November 2023).
5. S. L. Rodriguez and A. Kaur, "Understanding Computing Identity for Latina Students at a Hispanic-Serving Community College," *Journal of Hispanic Higher Education* (2024), https://doi.org/10.1177/153819272412782.
6. G. T. Doran, "There's a S.M.A.R.T. Way to Write Management's Goals and Objectives," *Management Review* 70, no. 11 (1981): 35–36.

Chapter 5

1. S. Cisneros, "A Woman of No Consequence/Una Mujer Cualquiera," in *Living Chicana Theory*, Series in Chicana/Latina Studies, ed. C. Trujillo (Bloomington, IN: Third Woman Press, 1998).
2. See, for example, S. L. Rodriguez, "Las Mujeres in the STEM Pipeline: How Latina College Students Who Persist in STEM Majors Develop and Sustain Their Science Identities" (PhD diss., 2015); S. L. Rodriguez et al., "Critiquing Oppression and Desiring Social Justice: How Undergraduate Latina Students in STEM Engage in Acts of Resistance," *Journal of Women and Gender in Higher Education* 13, no. 3 (2020): 251–67; S. L. Rodriguez, C. Lu, and D. Ramirez, "Creating a Conceptual Framework for Computing Identity Development for Latina Undergraduate Students," in *An Asset-Based Approach to Advancing Latina Students in STEM: Increasing Resilience, Participation, and Success*, ed. Elsa Gonzalez, Frank Fernandez, and Miranda Wilson (New York: Routledge, 2020), 25.
3. Rodriguez et al., "Critiquing Oppression and Desiring Social Justice."
4. N. Garza and S. Rodriguez, "Conocimientos and the Borderlands of Identity from Mexican American Women in Engineering and Computer Science" (paper presented at American Society for Engineering Education Annual Conference and Exposition, Minneapolis, MN, August 2022); N. E. Garza, S. L. Rodriguez, and M. L. Espino, "Nepantla aquí, Nepantla allá: The Borderlands of Identity from Mexican-Origin Women in STEM," *Journal of Hispanic Higher Education* 22, no. 2 (2023): 130–45.
5. Daisy Ramirez et al., "'I Started Seeing Myself as a Computing Person': Exploring Latina Women's Computing Identity Development in College," *Journal Committed to Social Change on Race and Ethnicity* 10, no. 2 (2024): 24–43; S. L. Rodriguez et al., "Utilizing Community Cultural Wealth to Explore the Experiences of Latina Undergraduate Students in Computing," *Journal of Women and Minorities in Science and Engineering* 29, no. 3 (2023): 1–24.
6. See, for example, Rodriguez, "Las Mujeres in the STEM Pipeline"; Rodriguez et al., "Critiquing Oppression and Desiring Social Justice."

Chapter 6

1. Cherríe Moraga, "La Güera," in *This Bridge Called My Back 40th Anniversary Edition*, ed. Cherríe Moraga and Gloria Anzaldúa (Albany: State University of New York Press, 2021), 29.
2. D. Ramirez et al., "'I Started Seeing Myself as a Computing Person': Exploring Latina Women's Computing Identity Development in College," *Journal Committed to Social Change on Race and Ethnicity* 10, no. 2 (2024): 23–43; S. Rodriguez, K. Cunningham, and A. Jordan, "STEM Identity Development for Latinas: The Role of Self- and Outside Recognition," *Journal of Hispanic Higher Education* 18, no. 3 (2019): 254–72; S. L. Rodriguez et al., "Utilizing Community Cultural Wealth to Explore the Experiences of Latina Undergraduate Students in Computing," *Journal of Women and Minorities in Science and Engineering* 29, no. 3 (2023): 1–24, https://doi.org/10.1615/JWomenMinorScienEng.2022039365.
3. Gloria Anzaldúa, "La Prieta," in *This Bridge Called My Back 40th Anniversary Edition*, ed. Cherríe Moraga and Gloria Anzaldúa (Albany: State University of New York Press, 2021).
4. Ramirez et al., "I Started Seeing Myself as a Computing Person"; S. L. Rodriguez et al., "Becoming la Ingeniera: Examining the Engineering Identity Development of Undergraduate Latina Students," *Journal of Latinos and Education* 21, no. 2 (2022): 181–200; S. L. Rodriguez et al., "Latina Undergraduate Students in STEM: The Role of Religious Beliefs and STEM Identity," *Journal of College and Character* 20, no. 1 (2019): 25–46, https://doi.org/10.1080/2194587X.2018.1559198.
5. Blanca Rincon and Sarah Rodriguez, "Latinx Students Charting Their Own STEM Pathways: How Community Cultural Wealth Informs Their STEM Identities," *Journal of Hispanic Higher Education* 20, no. 2 (2020), https://doi.org/10.1177/1538192720968276; S. L. Rodriguez and A. Stevens, "Exploring Computing Identity Development for Latinx Students at a Hispanic-Serving Community College," *Journal of Diversity in Higher Education* (2023), https://doi.org/10.1037/dhe0000530.
6. Toni Cade Bambara, "Foreword to the First Edition, 1981," in *This Bridge Called My Back 40th Anniversary Edition*, ed. Cherríe Moraga and Gloria Anzaldúa (Albany: State University of New York Press, 2021), xxxvii.
7. Derrick Bell, *Silent Covenants: Brown v. Board of Education and the Unfulfilled Hopes for Racial Reform* (New York: Oxford University Press, 2004); L. D. Baber, "Considering the Interest-Convergence Dilemma in STEM Education," *Review of Higher Education* 38, no. 2 (2015): 251–70.
8. S. L. Rodriguez, C. Lu, and D. Ramirez, "Navigating Operating Systems: A Framework for Understanding Identity Development for Undergraduate Latina Students in Computing," in *An Asset-Based Approach to Advancing Latina Students in STEM: Increasing Resilience, Participation, and Success*, ed. E. M. Gonzalez, F. Fernandez, and M. Wilson (London: Routledge, 2020).
9. Rodriguez and Stevens, "Exploring Computing Identity Development for Latinx Students at a Hispanic-Serving Community College"; S. L. Rodriguez and A. Kaur, "Understanding Latina Computing Identity Development at a Hispanic-Serving Community College" (paper presented at Association for the Study of Higher Education Annual Conference, Minneapolis, MN, November 2023); Ramirez et al., "I Started Seeing Myself as a Computing Person."
10. S. L. Rodriguez and A. Kaur, "Understanding Computing Identity for Latina Students at a Hispanic-Serving Community College," *Journal of Hispanic Higher Education* (2024), https://doi.org/10.1177/15381927241278299.

11. S. L. Rodriguez and J. M. Blaney, "'We're the Unicorns in STEM': Understanding How Academic and Social Experiences Influence Sense of Belonging for Latina Undergraduate Students," *Journal of Diversity in Higher Education* 14, no. 3 (2021): 441–55, https://doi.org/10.1037/dhe0000176; Sarah L. Rodriguez et al., "Critiquing Oppression and Desiring Social Justice: How Undergraduate Latinas in STEM Engage in Acts of Resistance," *NASPA Journal of Women and Gender in Higher Education* 13, no. 3 (2020): 251–67, https://doi.org/10.1080/26379112.2020.1838297.
12. S. L. Rodriguez et al., "Utilizing Community Cultural Wealth to Explore the Experiences of Latina Undergraduate Students in Computing."
13. Douglas Stone, Bruce Patton, and Sheila Heen, *Difficult Conversations: How to Discuss What Matters Most* (New York: Penguin, 2023); Kerry Patterson, Joseph Grenny, Ron McMillan, Al Switzler, Stephen R. Covey, and Laura Roppé, *Crucial Conversations* (Brilliance Audio, 2012).
14. Gloria Anzaldúa, "The New Mestiza Nation: A Multicultural Movement," in *The Gloria Anzaldúa Reader*, ed. Gloria Anzaldúa and AnaLouise Keating (Durham, NC: Duke University Press, 2009); K. D. Zaytoun, "'Now Let Us Shift' the Subject: Tracing the Path and Posthumanist Implications of La Naguala/The Shapeshifter in the Works of Gloria Anzaldúa," *MELUS* 40, no. 4 (2015): 69–88, http://www.jstor.org/stable/24569997.
15. Anzaldúa, "The New Mestiza Nation," 211.
16. Ramirez et al., "I Started Seeing Myself as a Computing Person."
17. S. L. Rodriguez. "Las Mujeres in the STEM Pipeline: How Latina College Students Who Persist in STEM Majors Develop and Sustain Their Science Identities" (PhD diss., 2015).
18. E. J. Abrica, "Revisiting the Complexity of Racial Understandings and Subjective Experiences of Race Among Students of Color in Stem Higher Education: Toward a Racial Reappraisal Framework," *Journal of Women and Minorities in Science and Engineering* 28, no. 2 (2022): 31–52, https://doi.org/10.1615/JWomenMinorScienEng.2022036573; L. Perez-Felkner, S. L. Rodriguez, and C. Fluker, *Latin* Students in Engineering: An Intentional Focus on a Growing Population* (New Brunswick, NJ: Rutgers University Press, 2024).
19. G. Q. Conchas and N. Acevedo, *The Chicana/o/x Dream: Hope, Resistance, and Educational Success* (Cambridge, MA: Harvard Education Press, 2020), 34.
20. A. Valenzuela, *Subtractive Schooling: US-Mexican Youth and the Politics of Caring* (Albany: State University of New York Press, 1999).
21. E. O. McGee, *Black, Brown, Bruised: How Racialized STEM Education Stifles Innovation* (Cambridge, MA: Harvard Education Press, 2021).
22. T. Okun, *White Supremacy Culture*, DRWorksBook, https://www.whitesupremacyculture.info/uploads/4/3/5/7/43579015/okun_-_white_sup_culture_2020.pdf.

Chapter 7

1. Gloria Anzaldúa, *Light in the Dark/Luz en lo Oscuro: Rewriting Identity, Spirituality, Reality* (Durham, NC: Duke University Press, 2015).
2. David Montejano, *Sancho's Journal: Exploring the Political Edge with the Brown Berets* (Austin: University of Texas Press, 2012).
3. "These States' Anti-DEI Legislation May Impact Higher Education," BestColleges.com, https://www.bestcolleges.com/news/anti-dei-legislation-tracker/#:~:text=As%20of%20May%202024%2C%2010,restricting%20DEI%20on%20college%20campuses.
4. Gloria E. Anzaldúa, "now let us shift . . . the path of conocimiento . . . inner work, public acts," in *this bridge we call home: radical visions for transformation*, ed. Gloria E. Anzaldúa and AnaLouise Keating (New York: Routledge, 2002), 571.

5. AnaLouise Keating, "From Borderlands and New Mestizas to Nepantlas and Nepantleras," *Human Architecture: Journal of the Sociology of Self-Knowledge* 4, no. 3 (2006): 5–16.
6. Sarah L. Rodriguez et al., "Critiquing Oppression and Desiring Social Justice: How Undergraduate Latinas in STEM Engage in Acts of Resistance," *NASPA Journal of Women and Gender in Higher Education* 13, no. 3 (2020): 251–67, https://doi.org/10.1080/26379112.2020.1838297.
7. Sarah L. Rodriguez et al., "Utilizing Community Cultural Wealth to Explore the Experiences of Latina Undergraduate Students in Computing," *Journal of Women and Minorities in Science and Engineering* 29, no. 3 (2023): 1–24, https://doi.org/10.1615/JWomenMinorScienEng.2022039365; S. L. Rodriguez and J. M. Blaney, "'We're the Unicorns in STEM': Understanding How Academic and Social Experiences Influence Sense of Belonging for Latina Undergraduate Students," *Journal of Diversity in Higher Education* 14, no. 3 (2020): 441–55, https://doi.org/10.1037/dhe0000176.
8. Blanca Rincon and Sarah Rodriguez, "Latinx Students Charting Their Own STEM Pathways: How Community Cultural Wealth Informs Their STEM Identities," *Journal of Hispanic Higher Education* 20, no. 2 (2020), https://doi.org/10.1177/1538192720968276.
9. Gloria E. Anzaldúa, *Borderlands/la Frontera: The New Mestiza* (San Francisco: Spinsters/Aunt Lute, 1987); Sosa-Provencio, Mia Angélica, Annmarie Sheahan, Shiv Desai, and Shawn Secatero, "Tenets of Body-Soul Rooted Pedagogy: Teaching for Critical Consciousness, Nourished Resistance, and Healing," *Critical Studies in Education* 61, no. 3 (2020): 345–62.
10. Robert J. Downey, Joel Alejandro Mejia, Diana A. Chen, and Gordon D. Hoople, "Meritocracy and Colorblindness: The Perpetuation of Whiteness in Engineering Education Through False Narratives" (presented at the American Society for Engineering Education Conference, Portland, OR, 2024); Tomoko M. Nakajima, Julia Rose Karpicz, and Justin A. Gutzwa, "'Why Isn't This Space More Inclusive?': Marginalization of Racial Equity Work in Undergraduate Computing Departments," *Journal of Diversity in Higher Education* 17, no. 1 (2024): 27.
11. Nolan L. Cabrera, "'Never Forget' the History of Racial Oppression: Whiteness, White Immunity, and Educational Debt in Higher Education," *Change: The Magazine of Higher Learning* 52, no. 2 (2020): 37–40, https://doi.org/10.1080/00091383.2020.1732774; Nolan L. Cabrera and Chris Corces-Zimmerman, "Beyond 'Privilege': Whiteness as the Center of Racial Marginalization," in *Marginality in the Urban Center: The Costs and Challenges of Continued Whiteness in the Americas and Beyond*, ed. Peary Brug, Zachary S. Ritter, and Kenneth R. Roth (New York: Palgrave Macmillan, 2019), 13–29; James Holly and Stephanie Masta, "Making Whiteness Visible: The Promise of Critical Race Theory in Engineering Education," *Journal of Engineering Education* 110, no. 4 (2021): 798–802, https://doi.org/10.1002/jee.20432; F. W. Twine, "Whiteness as a Form of Geek Capital in Silicon Valley," in *The Routledge International Handbook of New Critical Race and Whiteness Studies*, ed. Rikke Andreassen et al. (New York: Routledge, 2023), 27–43.
12. E. Gutierrez et al., "Whiteness: White Privilege, White Supremacy, and White Fragility," *ASCCC Open Educational Resources Initiative (OERI)*, https://socialsci.libretexts.org/Bookshelves/Social_Justice_Studies/Race_and_Ethnic_Relations_in_the_U.S.%3A_An_Intersectional_Approach/06%3A_Euro_Americans_and_Whiteness/6.03%3A_Whiteness-__White_Privilege_White_Supremacy_and_White_Fragility; Downey et al., "Meritocracy and Colorblindness"; Nakajima et al., "Why Isn't This Space More Inclusive?"

13. P. McIntosh, "White Privilege: Unpacking the Invisible Knapsack," *Peace and Freedom Magazine*, July/August 1989, 10–12.
14. T. Okun, "White Supremacy Culture – Still Here," 2021, https://www.dismantlingracism.org/uploads/4/3/5/7/43579015/white_supremacy_culture_-_still_here.pdf.
15. R. DiAngelo, *White Fragility: Why It's So Hard for White People to Talk About Racism* (Boston: Beacon, 2018).
16. AnaLouise Keating, "Shifting Perspectives: Spiritual Activism, Social Transformation, and the Politics of Spirit," in *EntreMundos/AmongWorlds: New Perspectives on Gloria E. Anzaldúa* (New York: Palgrave Macmillan, 2005), 241–54.
17. Anzaldúa, "now let us shift," 1.
18. C. Elenes, "Nepantla, Spiritual Activism, New Tribalism: Chicana Feminist Transformative Pedagogies and Social Justice Education," *Journal of Latino/Latin American Studies* 5, no. 3 (2013): 136.
19. M. Salazar Pérez and C. M. Saavedra, "Spiritual Activism as a Means for Social Transformation: Womanist and Chicana Feminist Possibilities," *Equity and Excellence in Education* 53, no. 3 (2020): 315–23.
20. Mia Angélica Sosa-Provencio, Annmarie Sheahan, Shiv Desai, and Shawn Secatero, "Tenets of Body-Soul Rooted Pedagogy: Teaching for Critical Consciousness, Nourished Resistance, and Healing," *Critical Studies in Education* 61, no. 3 (2020): 345–62.
21. Gloria E. Anzaldúa, *Light in the Dark*; D. Calderón, "Anticolonial Methodologies in Education: Embodying Land and Indigeneity in Chicana Feminisms," *Journal of Latino/Latin American Studies* 6, no. 2 (2014): 81–96; C. Cruz, "Toward an Epistemology of a Brown Body," in *Chicana/Latina Education in Everyday Life: Feminista Perspectives on Pedagogy and Epistemology*, ed. D. Delgado Bernal, C. A. Elenes, F. E. Godinez, and S. Villenas (Albany: State University of New York Press, 2006), 59–75; K. Pendleton Jiménez, "Start with the Land: Groundwork for Chicana Pedagogy," in *Chicana/Latina Education in Everyday Life: Feminista Perspectives on Pedagogy and Epistemology*, ed. D. Delgado Bernal, C. A. Elenes, F. E. Godinez, and S. Villenas (Albany: State University of New York Press, 2006), 219–29.
22. Dolores Delgado Bernal, "Using a Chicana Feminist Epistemology in Educational Research," *Harvard Educational Review* 68, no. 4 (1998): 555–83.
23. Teresa Córdova, "Roots and Resistance: The Emergent Writings of Twenty Years of Chicana Feminist Struggle," *Handbook of Hispanic Cultures in the United States: Sociology* 3 (1994): 175–202.
24. Anzaldúa, "now let us shift."

Chapter 8

1. Cherríe Moraga and Gloria Anzaldúa, "El Mundo Zurdo," in *This Bridge Called My Back, Fortieth Anniversary Edition: Writings by Radical Women of Color*, ed. Cherríe Moraga and Gloria Anzaldúa (Albany: State University of New York Press, 2021), 195–96.

Acknowledgments

First and foremost, I want to thank all the Latina college students who have taken the time to share their stories with me. *Mujer,* I see you. I see your triumphs and your challenges. I see you working day in and day out to make a place for yourself in engineering and computing. I have seen you go on to become engineers and computer scientists, and every time, my heart bursts with pride—you are the manifestation of our ancestors' dreams. I would also like to acknowledge all the equity-minded practitioners who have helped guide me over the years, both inspiring me and challenging me to think about what is possible and what our responsibility is to the students we serve. Every time that I felt like shelving this project, I thought of you. Without you, none of this would be possible, and I am forever indebted to you for the work that you do. In this spirit, I also want to express my gratitude for all the Chicana feminist writers and activists upon whose work this book builds. Standing on the shoulders of giants does not even begin to cover it. It is your spirit that sustained me throughout this book-writing process.

Writing a book is hard, y'all. From first thought to final proofs, this project spanned a pandemic, a baby, two career moves, eight housing moves, and a change in professional fields (higher education to engineering education)—all in just a few short years. The number of tears cried and expletives muttered cannot be overestimated. Above all, this was a labor of absolute love. Writing is not a singular act; it is a practice, a craft, in which you must invest over and over. With every early morning, every cup of tea, and every deep breath and exhale, I brought myself back to the writing with tenderness and care. It was worth it because this work matters.

For helping to make this dream a reality, I must thank my Harvard Education Press editor, Karen Adler, for her unwavering patience as I wrote, stopped, and wrote again. Your feedback and belief in my work gave me the ability to keep moving forward, even through all of life's many transitions. I would also be remiss if I did not thank my long-time writing consultant, Danielle LaVaque-Manty, who has been with me since I became a professor. Your feedback has transformed my work and inspired me in countless ways.

However, before the inception of this book, there was me—the Latina student and budding writer. I must acknowledge my mentors who poured their time, love, and energy into me and my writing over the years: Vicki GoDair, Mandy Rolison, Jeremy McMillen, Gerald Duchovnay, Mark Reid, Margaret Sallee, Kay McClenney, and many more. From Nicole Guidotti-Hernández, who first introduced me to Chicana feminism, to Michelle Camacho and Norma Cantú, whose work on Latinas as STEM students touched off an entire research agenda for me—thank you for forging the way. A huge thank you to Victor Saenz, my former dissertation chair and now colleague and friend. You empowered me to get a certificate in Mexican American Studies and to forge my own Latina scholar identity. That seed you planted about identity continues to bear fruit, both personally and professionally, and I cannot thank you enough.

This book and my trajectory into engineering and computing education would not have been possible without the *ever* so patient mentorship of Marlene Strathe, Bob Reason, Lorenzo Baber, Diane Rover, Mani Mina, Craig Ogilvie, Linda Sax, Antonio Delgado, Nandika D'souza, Xueli Wang, Marilyn Amey, and all my National Science Foundation grant collaborators. You all taught me what good partnerships and meaningful work look like. Thank you to Beth Bukoski and Charles Lu, who have been with me for every step of the journey to this book, providing feedback and encouraging me to "name the baby" of racism, sexism, and other oppressions as well as make recommendations that are actionable for practitioners. A huge thank you to my various writing buddies over the years—Daniel Spikes, Rosie Perez, Kristina Maruyama Tank, Erin Doran, Shannon Coleman, Kevin McClure, Jorge Burmicky, Catherine Hartman, Rachel Friedensen, Amanda Morales, Crystal Garcia, Marissa Vasquez, Cris Salinas, Jennie Blaney, Blanca Rincón, and many more—who have scheduled regular coffee shop writing times, organized writing retreats, and generally kept me writing, even when I could barely eek out words. Special shout-out to all my #ChingonaScholars out there doing the work, but particularly Courtney Luedke and Elvira Abrica, who read drafts of this book and challenged me with every word to dig deeper, push harder, and tell the story more effectively. Thank you to my Virginia Tech mentors and colleagues—in particular, Susan Sajadi, Walt

Lee, David Knight, and Jenni Case—who have supported me as I navigated my transition within the engineering and computing education worlds. On days when I wasn't feeling the writing or just needed perspective, y'all provided. Y'all have made Virginia Tech a home. To my research team—the Rodriguez Research Group (RRG) members, past and present—thank you for all that you have done collecting, analyzing, coauthoring, and copresenting. Y'all make magic happen. Y'all breathed life into the work, and I am forever grateful.

Beyond the academic realm, it takes a village to write a book. Without my husband, Troy Jones, I could not have finished this book, plain and simple. You've been a part of my life for almost twenty years, and I consider myself the lucky one. You are the best partner that an academic could ask for. You encouraged me to take time to write but also reminded me when I needed a break to care for myself. While I toiled away early mornings at my keyboard or hid away from everyone else, you were there, ensuring that our daughter, Azalea, was equipped with an arsenal of snacks and that I had someone to vent to about my writing struggles. You keep me rooted in what is important but empower me to realize my dreams. Because of you, this dream became a reality.

I also want to thank my mother, Donna Goodell, for her continuous reminder that my book "isn't going to write itself" and her unwavering support over the years in all my endeavors. I got my tenacity from you, Mom. You always found a way—despite any obstacle. You were my first teacher of feminism and equity, and I owe much to you. Whether it's a macaroni wreath or a full-length academic press book, it makes no difference. If my mom is proud of me, that's what counts. Also thank you to my dads, Gilbert Rodriguez and Bryan Kanagy, for encouraging me to dream big and have fun throughout the process. Y'all have taught me so much about what it means to live and pursue my dreams in tandem. This book is possible because of those teachings. To my best friend of all time, Morgan Nichols, who has for twenty-five years brought laughter and light into my life, I thank you. You made my dreams of writing this book in the French countryside come true, and I am forever grateful. Everyone needs a best friend like you.

I would also like to take a page from Snoop Dogg and take the time to thank myself. I thank myself for believing in me, for holding myself accountable, and for putting in the time. And, for anyone who knows me well, you *know* that I found inspiration during this book-writing process from my favorite rappers

Trina and Sno Tha Product. In finishing this book, I truly feel like a Million Dollar Girl, you know, because That's My Attitude, and after all, I'm Still Da Baddest. I'm On My Sh*t, cuz that's How I Do It. Especially as I wrote that chapter on resistance, I tried to channel that energy. But, I digress. I hope that you enjoy this labor of love and find value in the words ahead.

About the Author

Sarah L. Rodriguez, PhD (she/her/hers), is an Associate Professor of Engineering Education and an affiliate faculty member with the Higher Education Program at Virginia Tech. Dr. Rodriguez is one of the nation's leading experts on Latina/o/x/e STEM (science, technology, engineering, and mathematics) students and was coeditor of the award-winning landmark book, *Latin* Students in Engineering: An Intentional Focus on a Growing Population*. Broadly, her work centers on STEM environments and identity development for historically marginalized populations at higher education institutions. She concentrates on identifying and asking urgent questions about systemic inequities such as racism, sexism, and classism that marginalized communities experience as they transition to and through their STEM education experiences. In particular, she has spent the last decade devoted to understanding and taking action to enhance the educational journeys of Latina engineering and computing students, who continue to be at the heart of her work.

Over the years, Dr. Rodriguez has been involved with several large-scale interdisciplinary research projects centered on institutional environments and STEM identity development, totaling over twenty million dollars, which have been sponsored by the National Science Foundation (NSF), the Kapor Center, and the Center for the Study of Community Colleges. Her work is featured in scholarly outlets such as *The Review of Higher Education*, *The Journal of Diversity in Higher Education*, and *The Journal of Women and Minorities in Science and Engineering*, as well as in popular and policy-based media outlets such as *Hispanic Outlook* and Education Commission of the States' *Strong Start to Finish Series*. For her work, Dr. Rodriguez received the 2025 Collaborative Network for Engineering and Computing Diversity (CoNECD) Rising Star in Diversity Award and the 2025 Women in Engineering Pro-Active Network (WEPAN) Betty Vetter Award for Research.

She received her PhD in higher education leadership and a certificate in Mexican American Studies from the University of Texas at Austin and holds a master's degree with a focus in college student personnel from the University of Tennessee. She holds a bachelor's degree in English and Spanish from Texas A&M University–Commerce and was a transfer student from Trinity Valley Community College. She is also a proud Bill and Melinda Gates Millennium Scholars (GMS) Program alum, born and raised in rural east Texas with family roots in the Rio Grande Valley. In her free time, she enjoys primitive camping with her family, being a "world traveler" as her Paw-Paw would say, and enjoying a glass of red wine. To learn more, visit http://sarahlrodriguez.com/.

Index